hello,

first, welcome to your colourimg book, and thank u for your order,

now you can color your mood with amazing colors pictures, and a

fucking amazing quotes. I made for you a different type of pictures

and motivational quotes to color it. if you like this book do not forget

to let your comment and stars

START YOUR DAY WITH COLORS ,

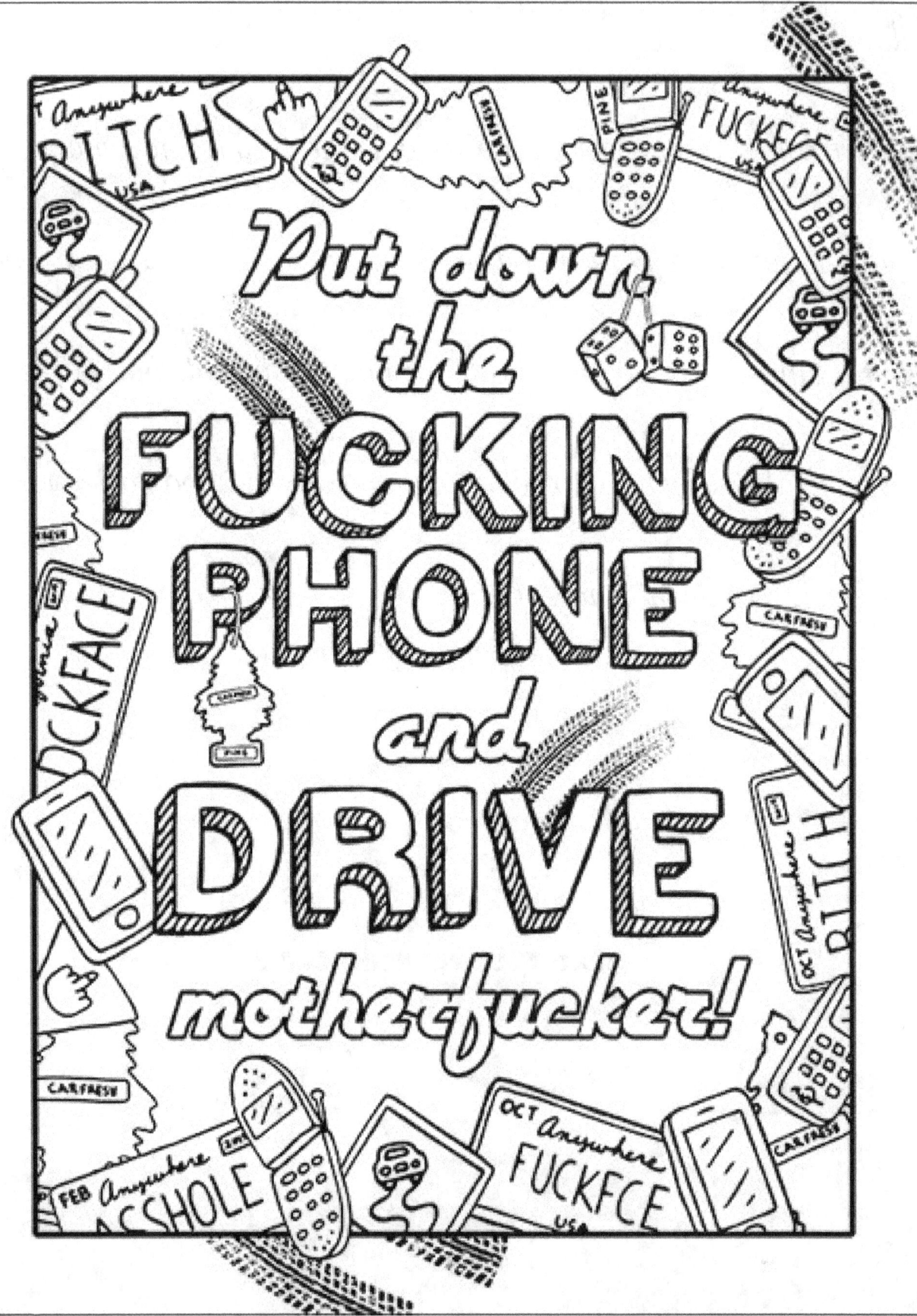

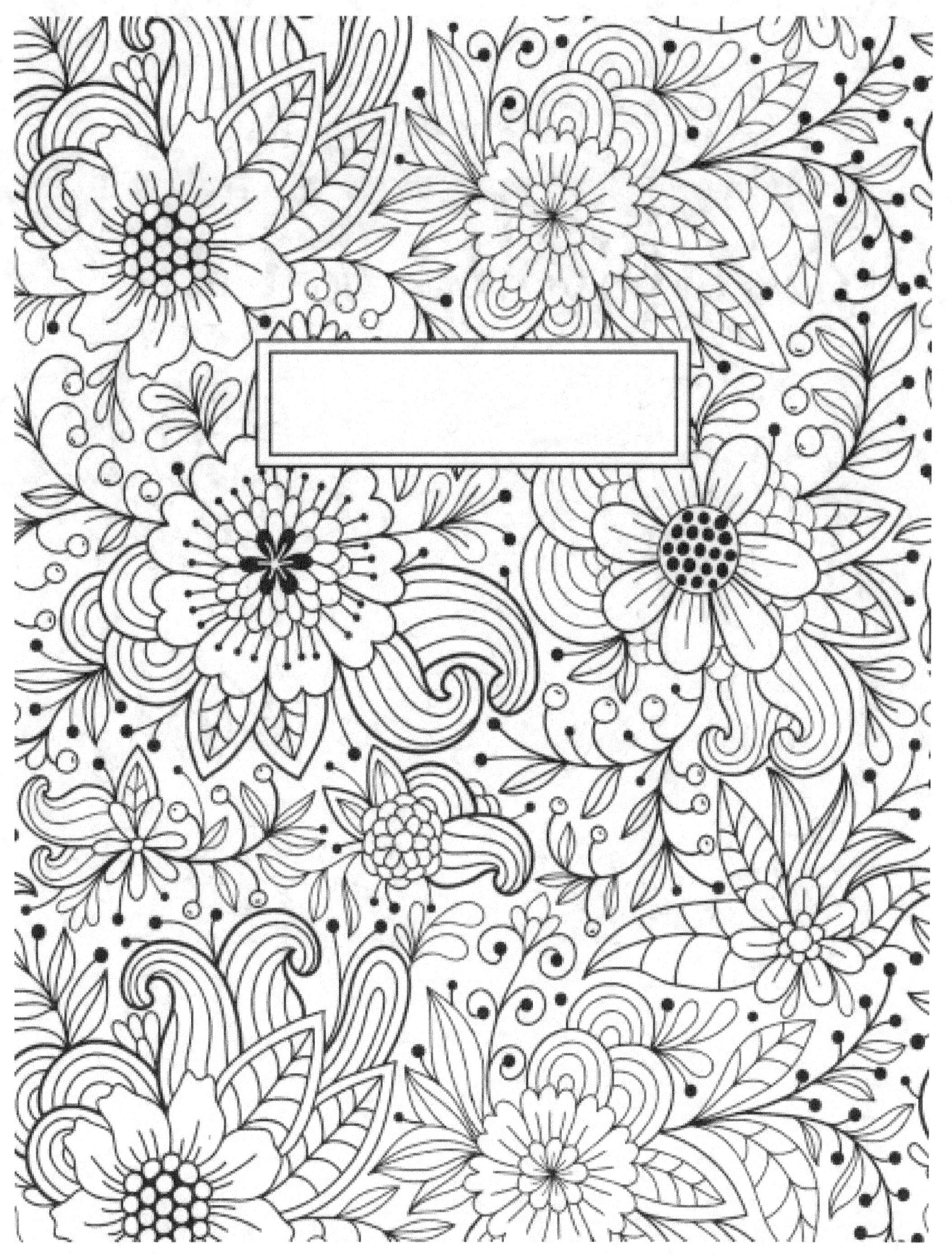

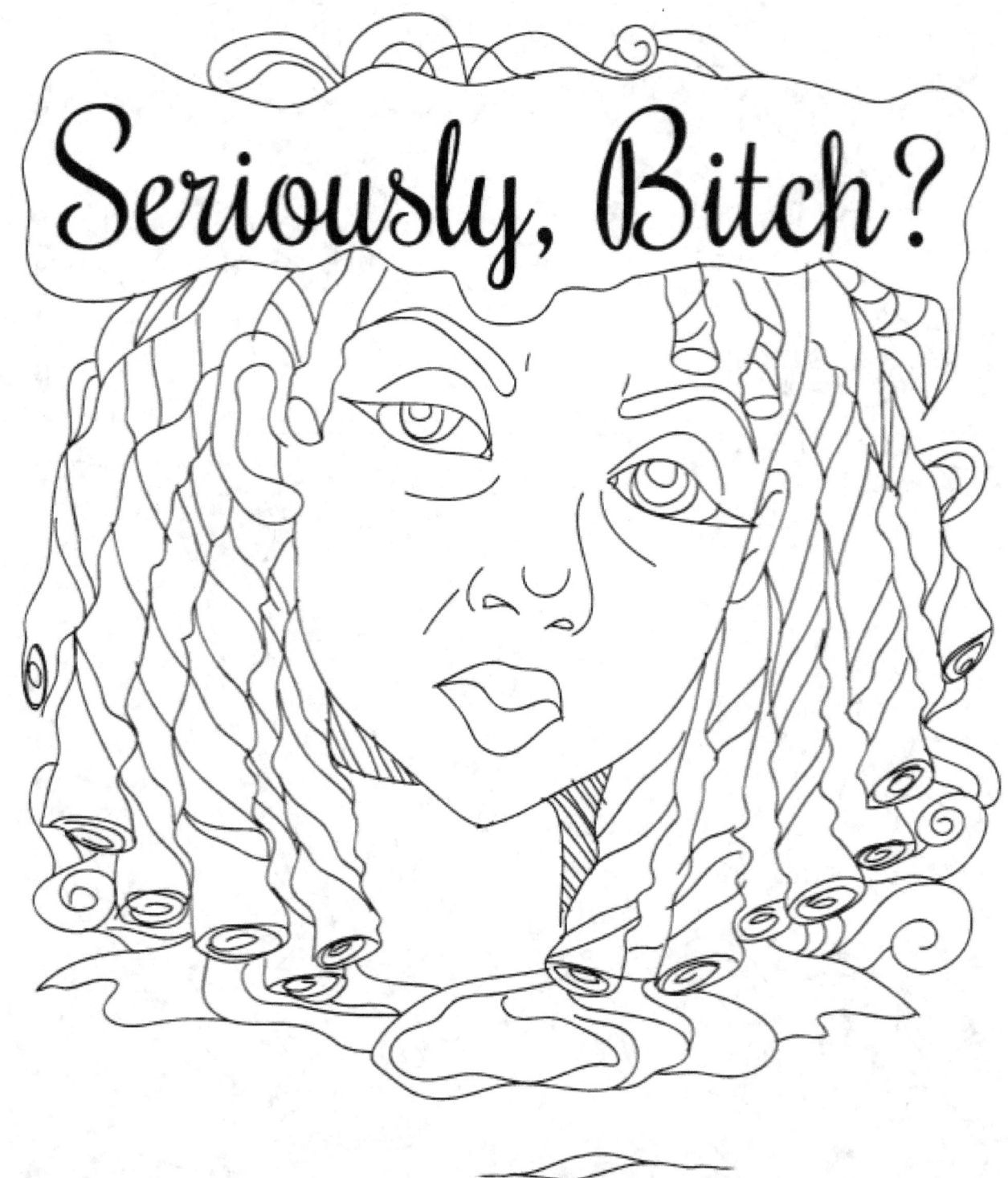

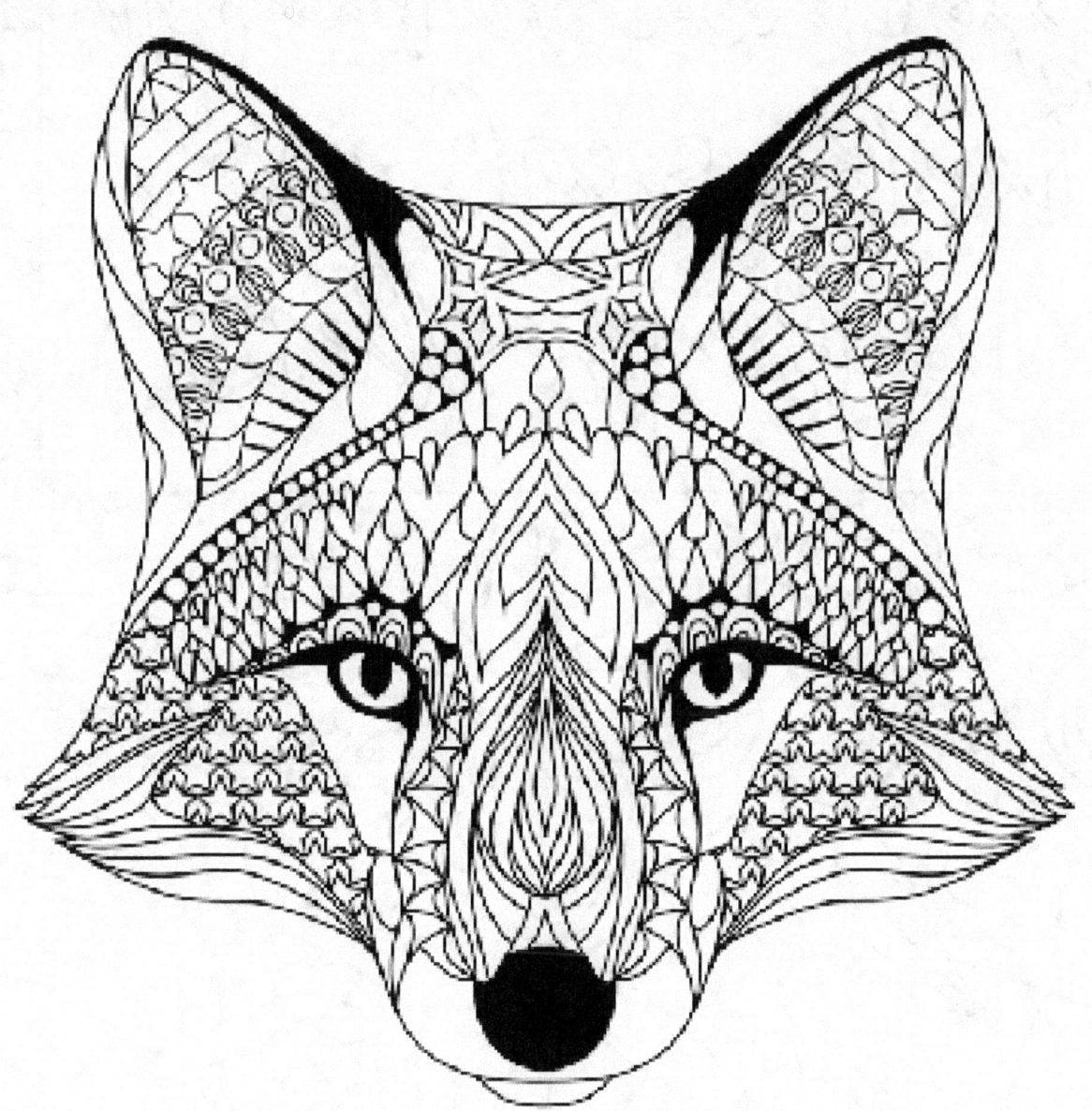

FUCK IT ?...

You were born to be real, not to be perfect

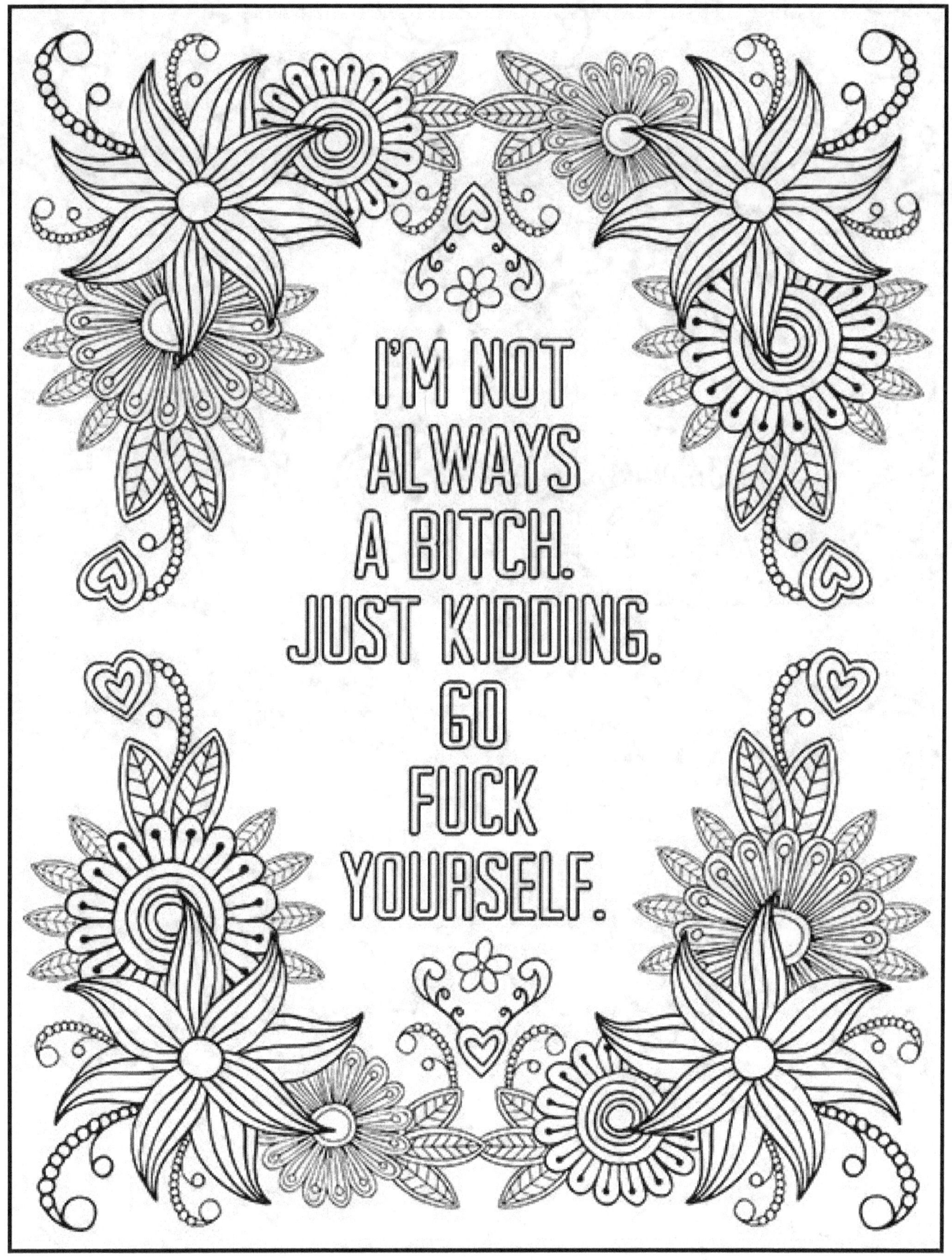

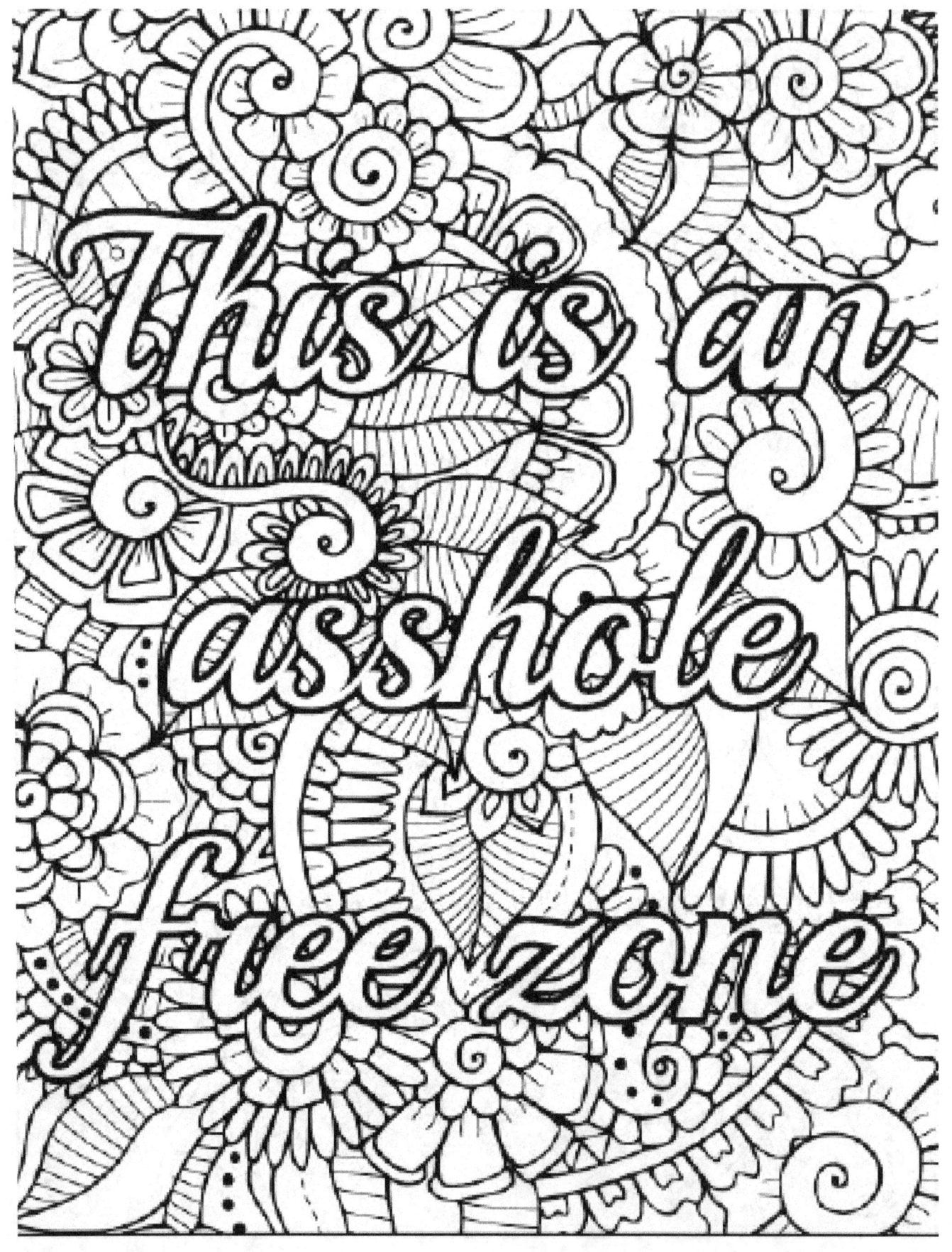

Fuck this Shit

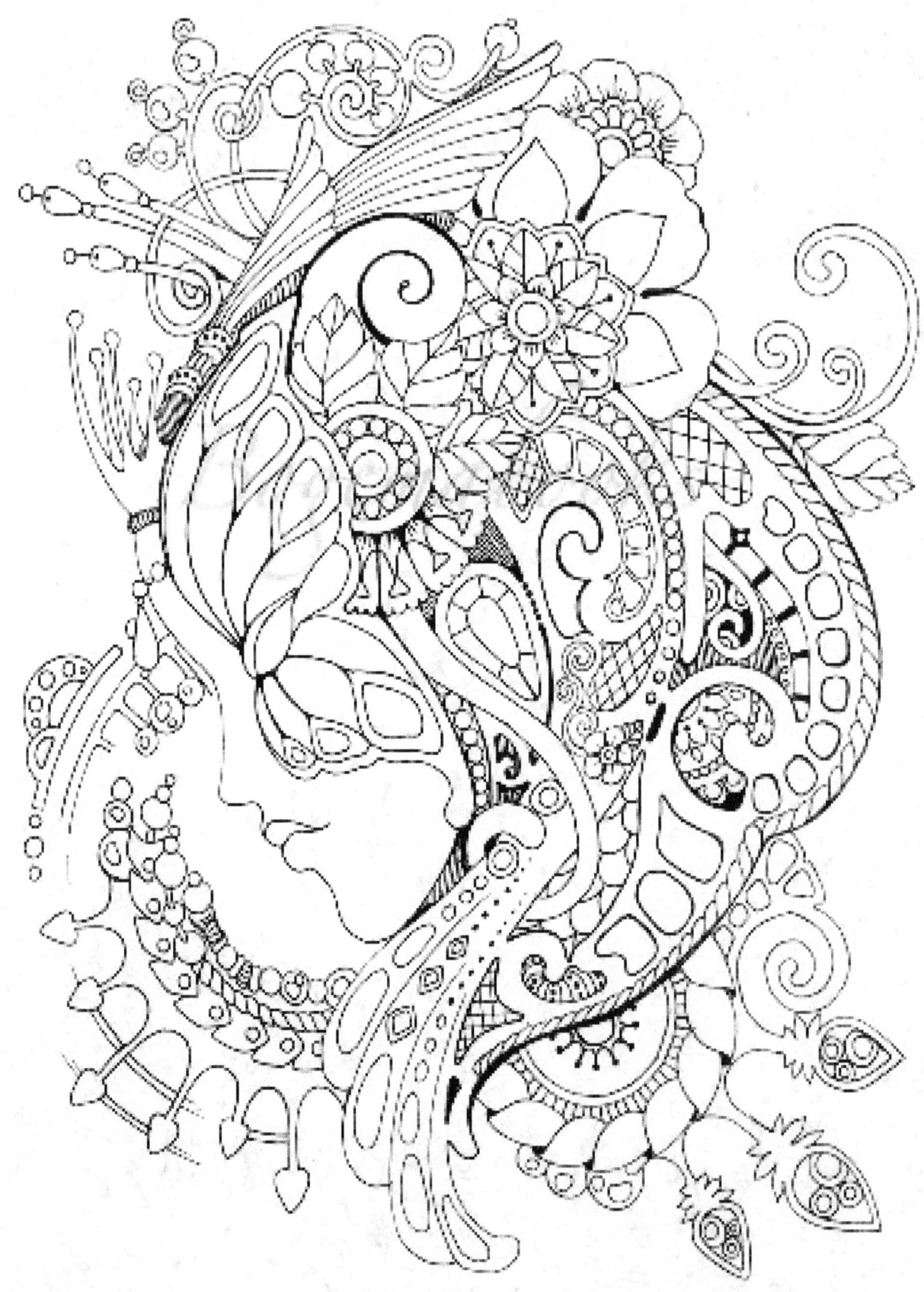

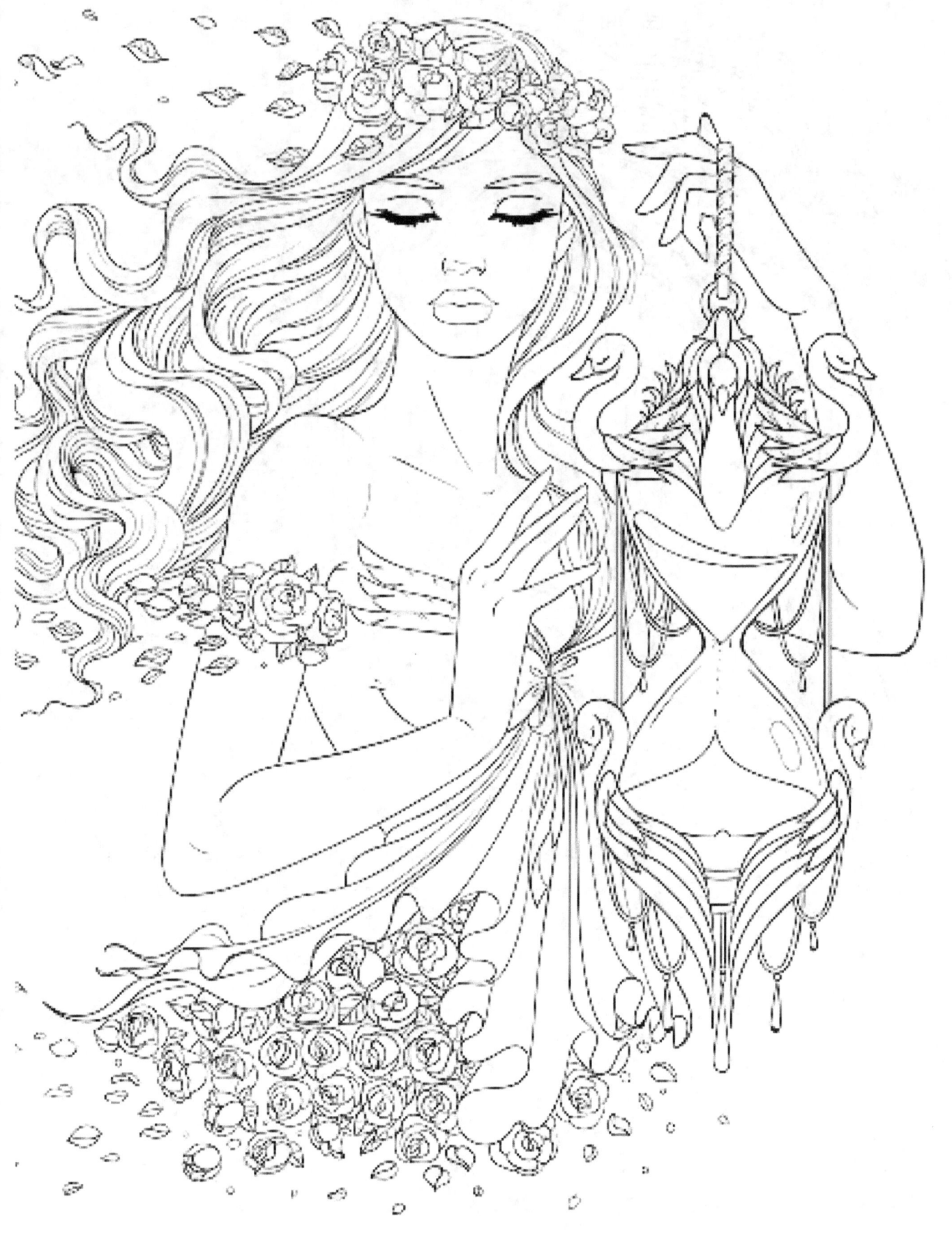

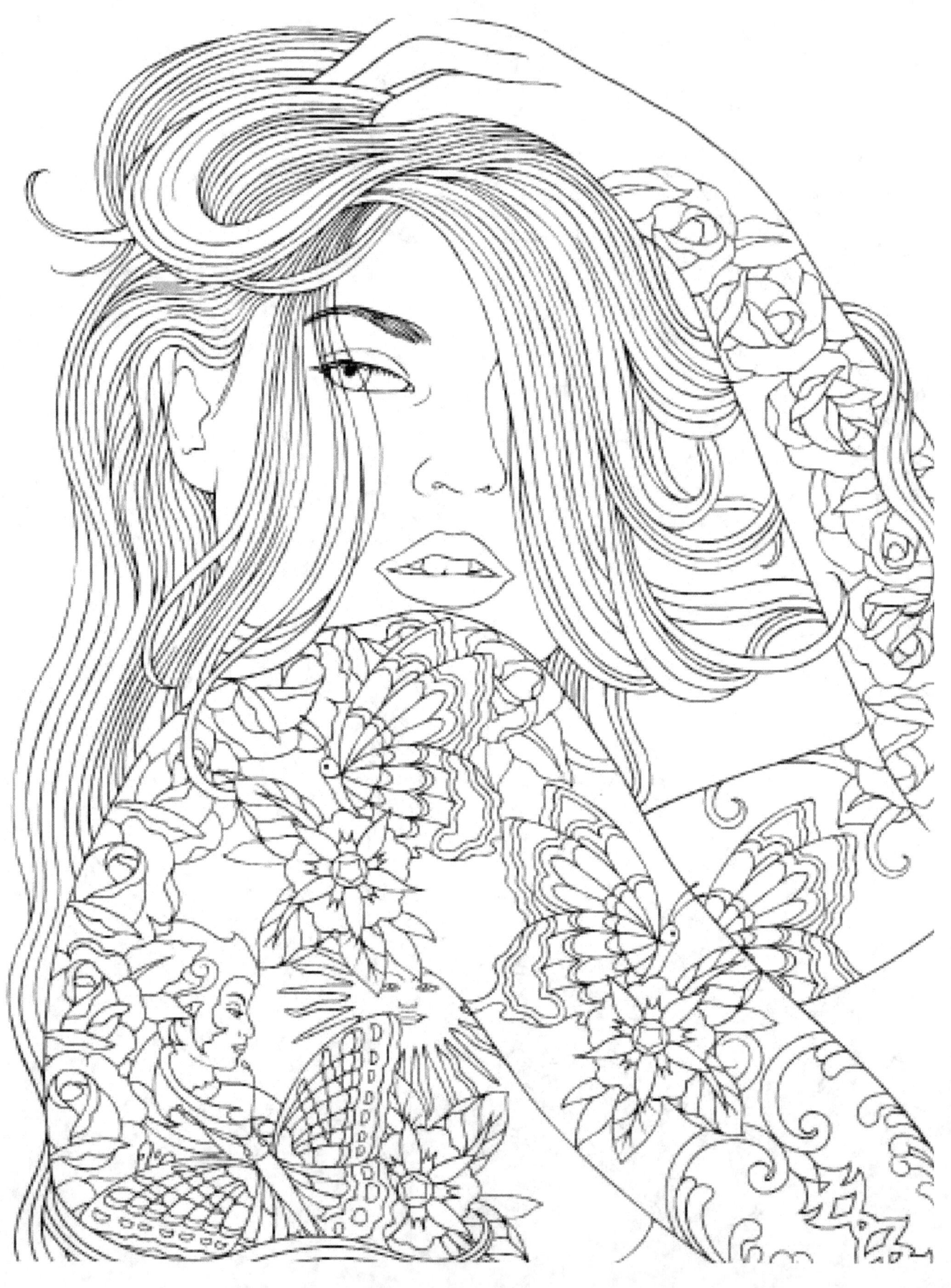

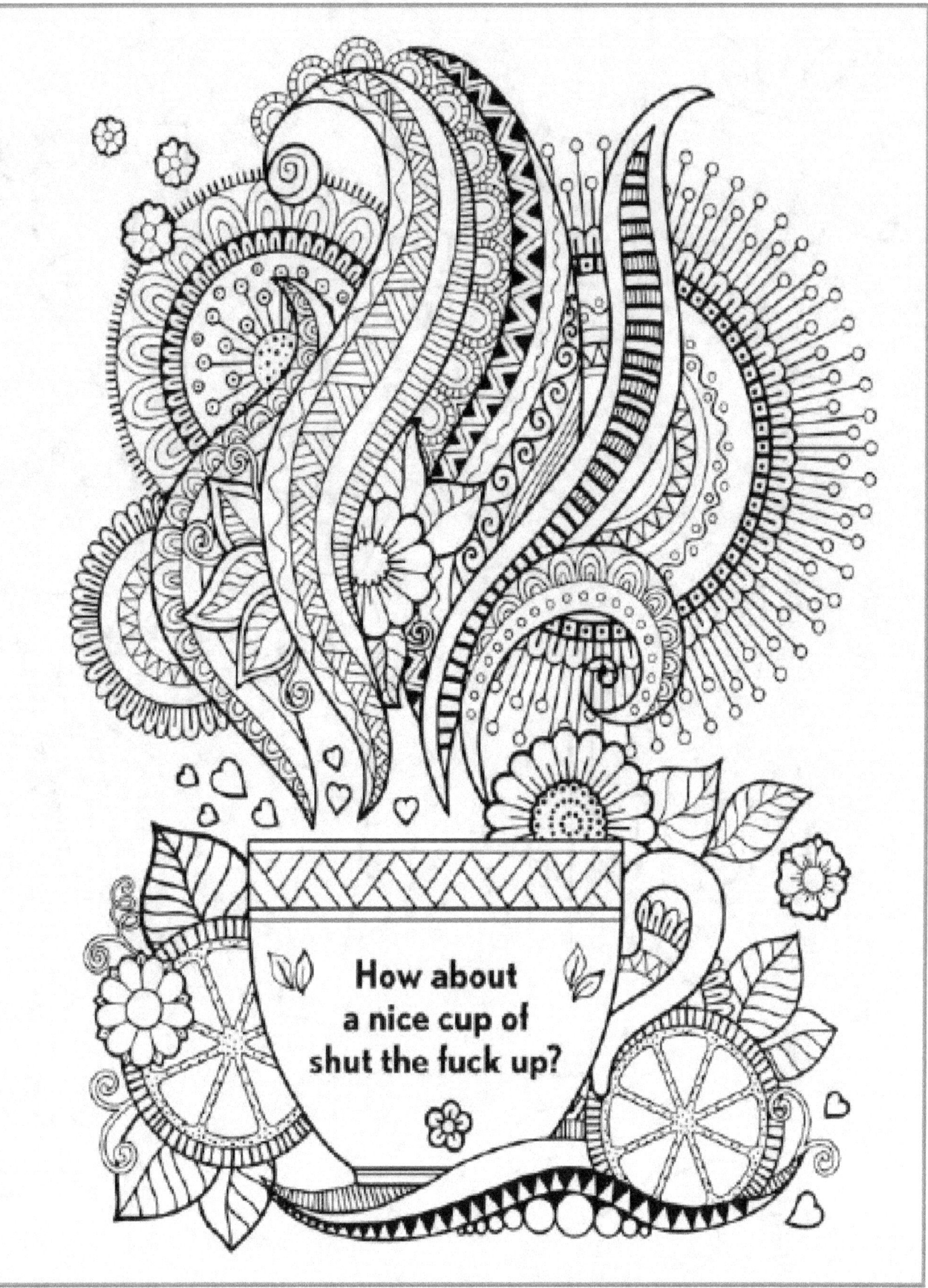

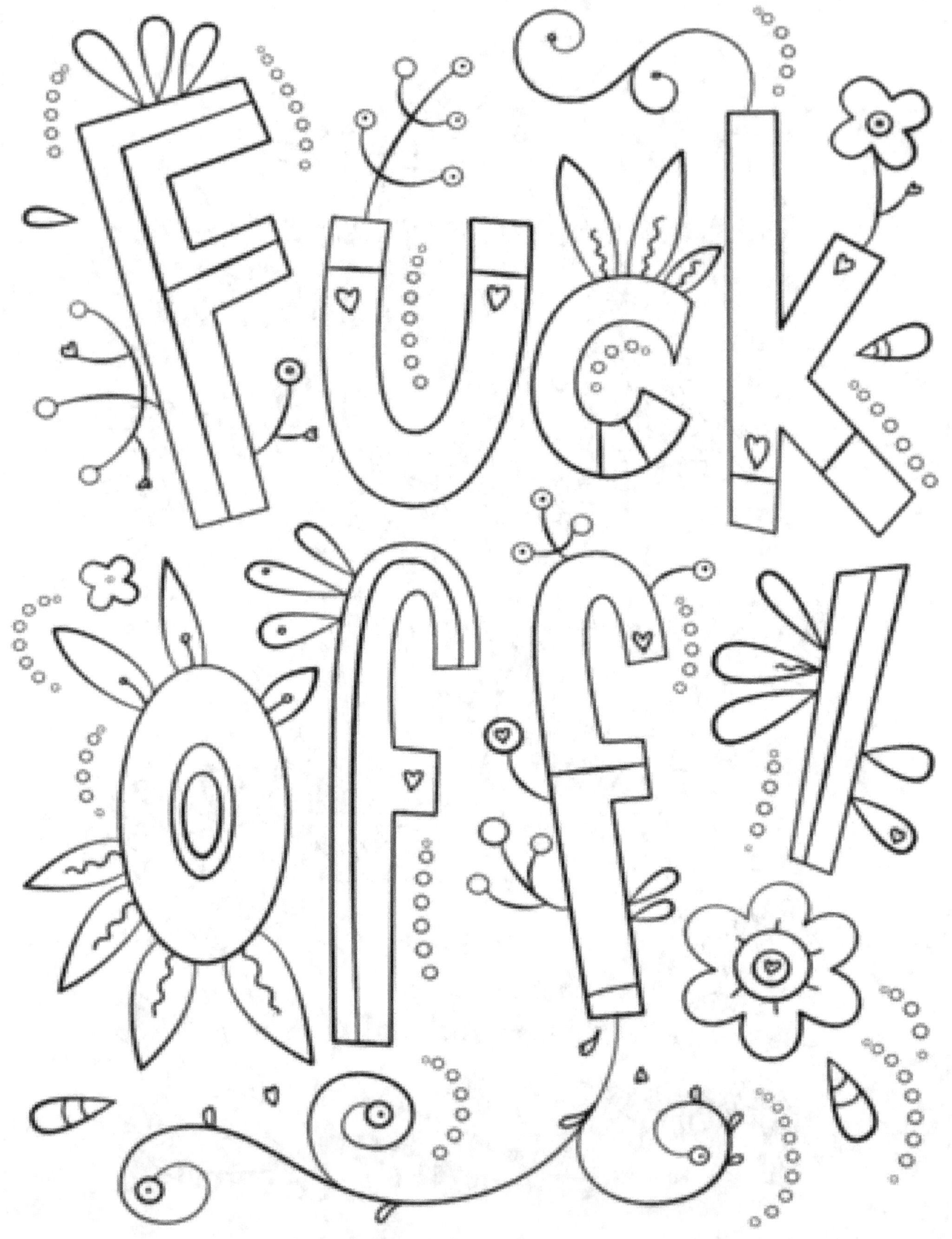

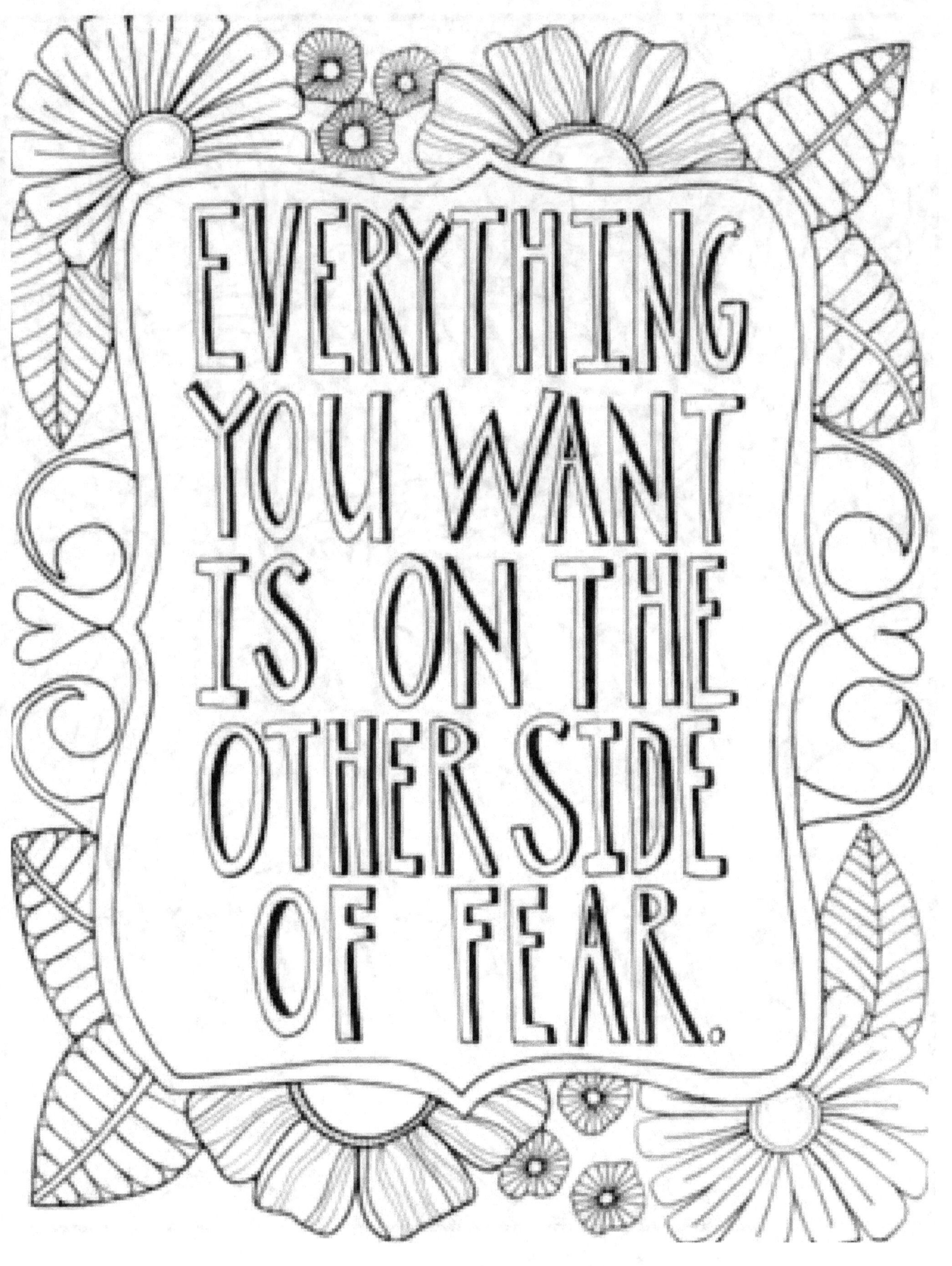

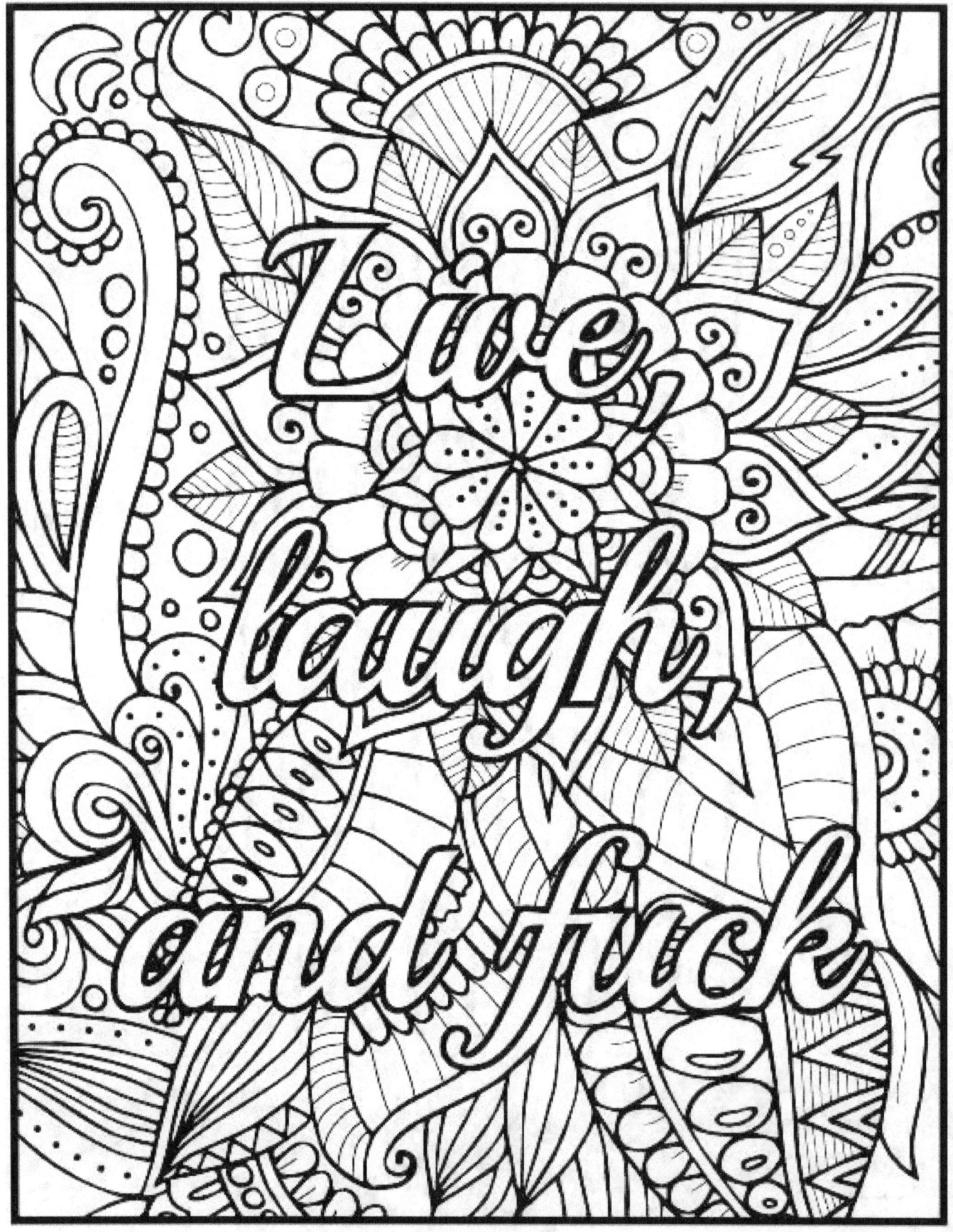

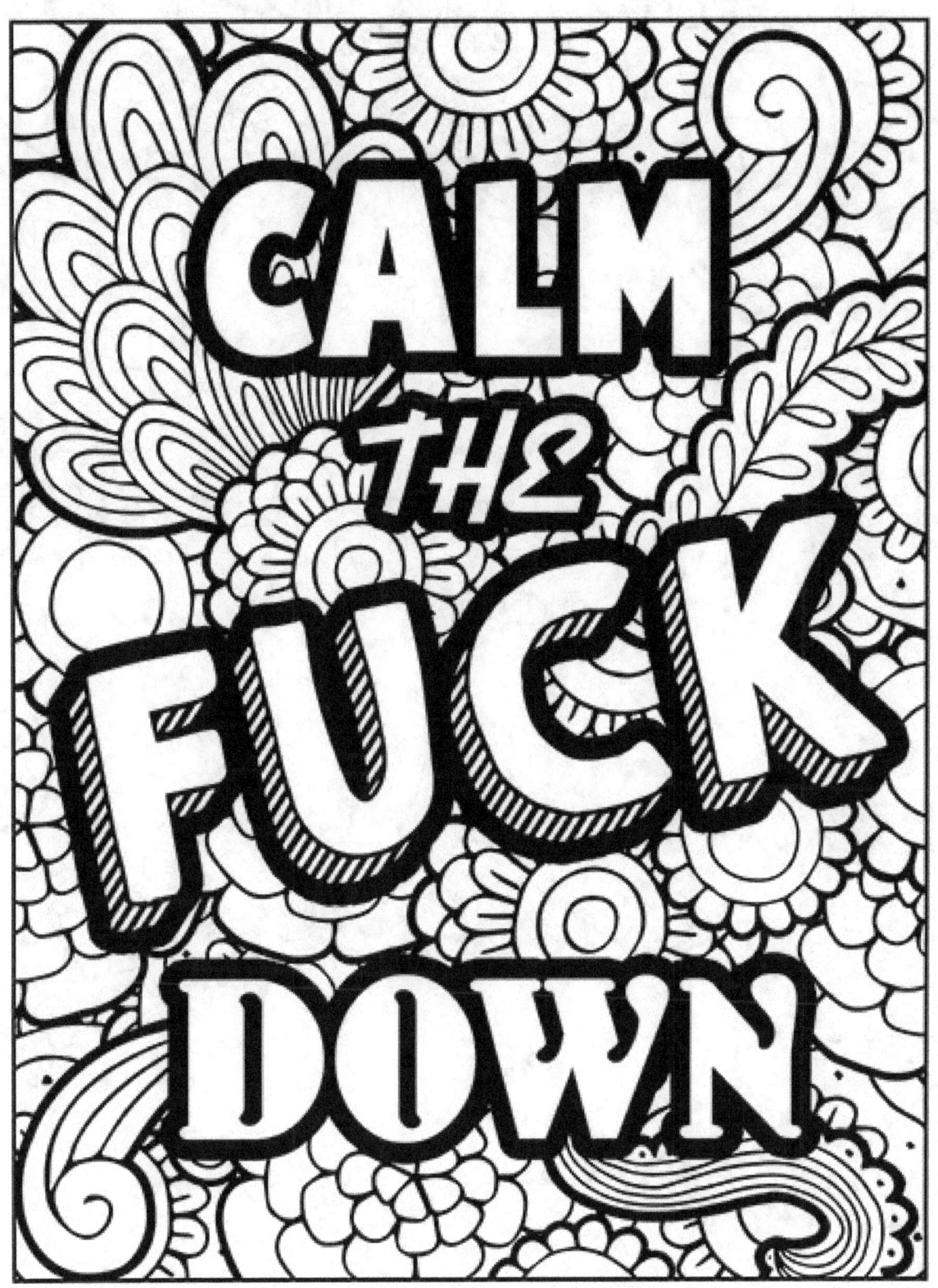

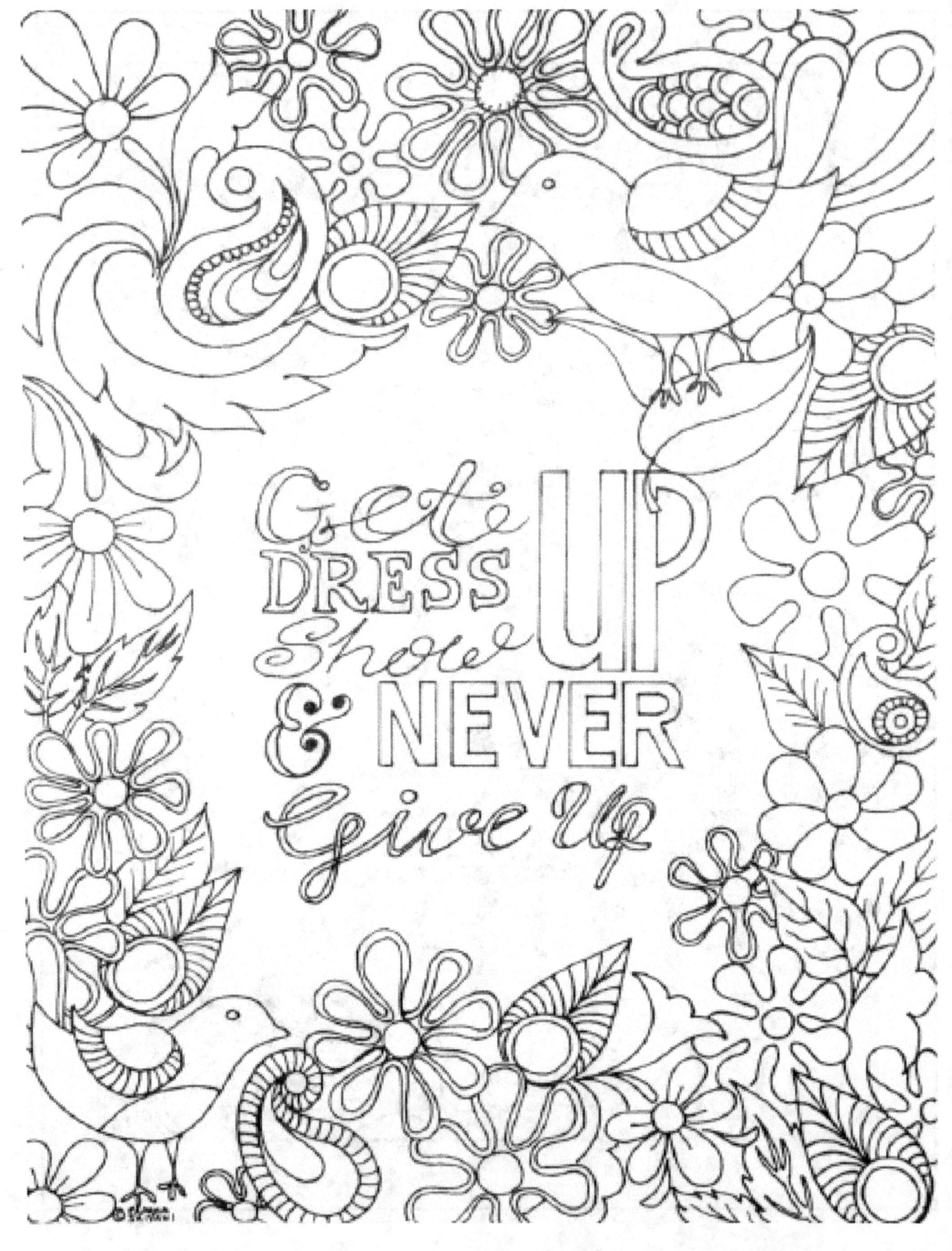

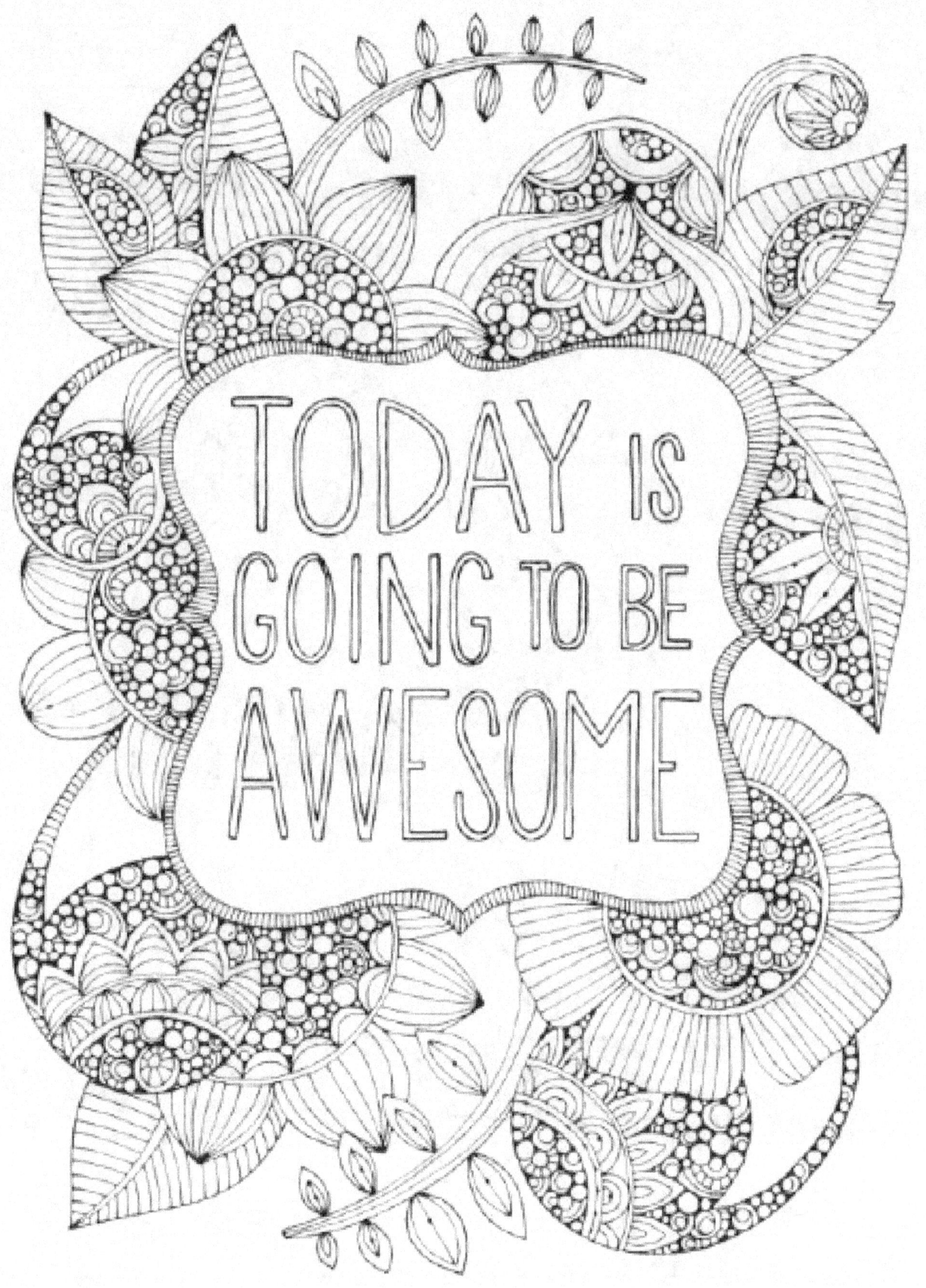

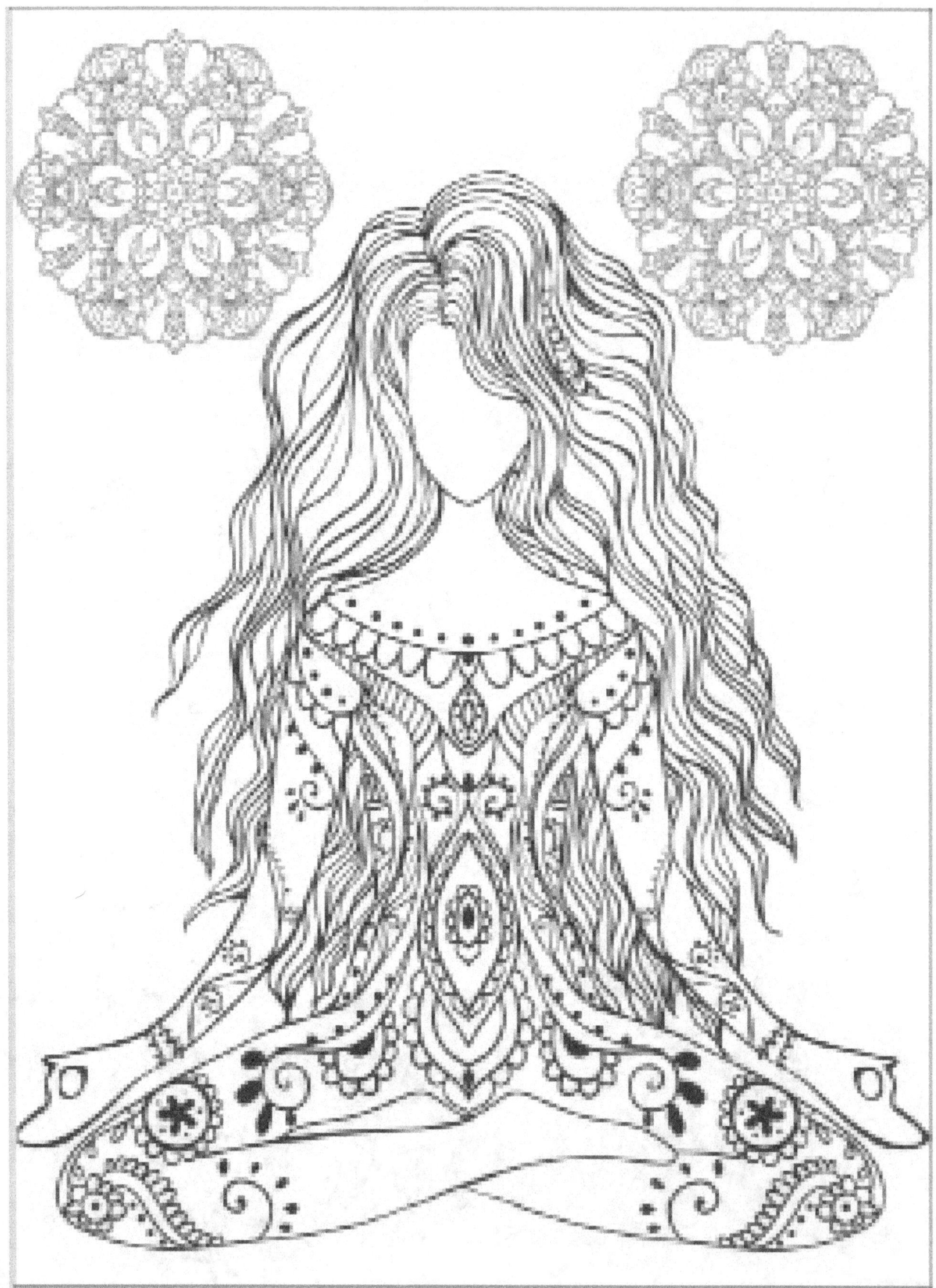

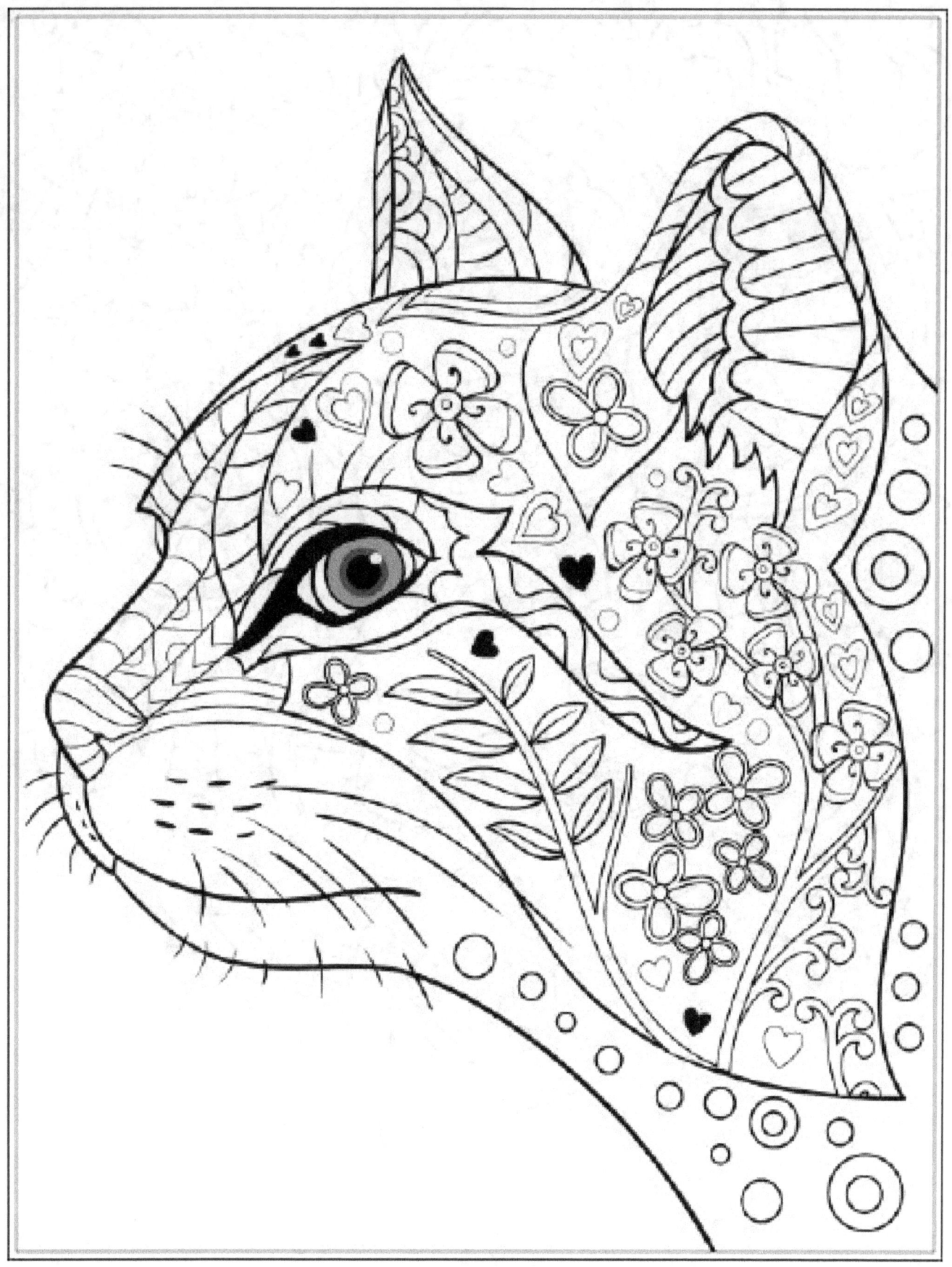

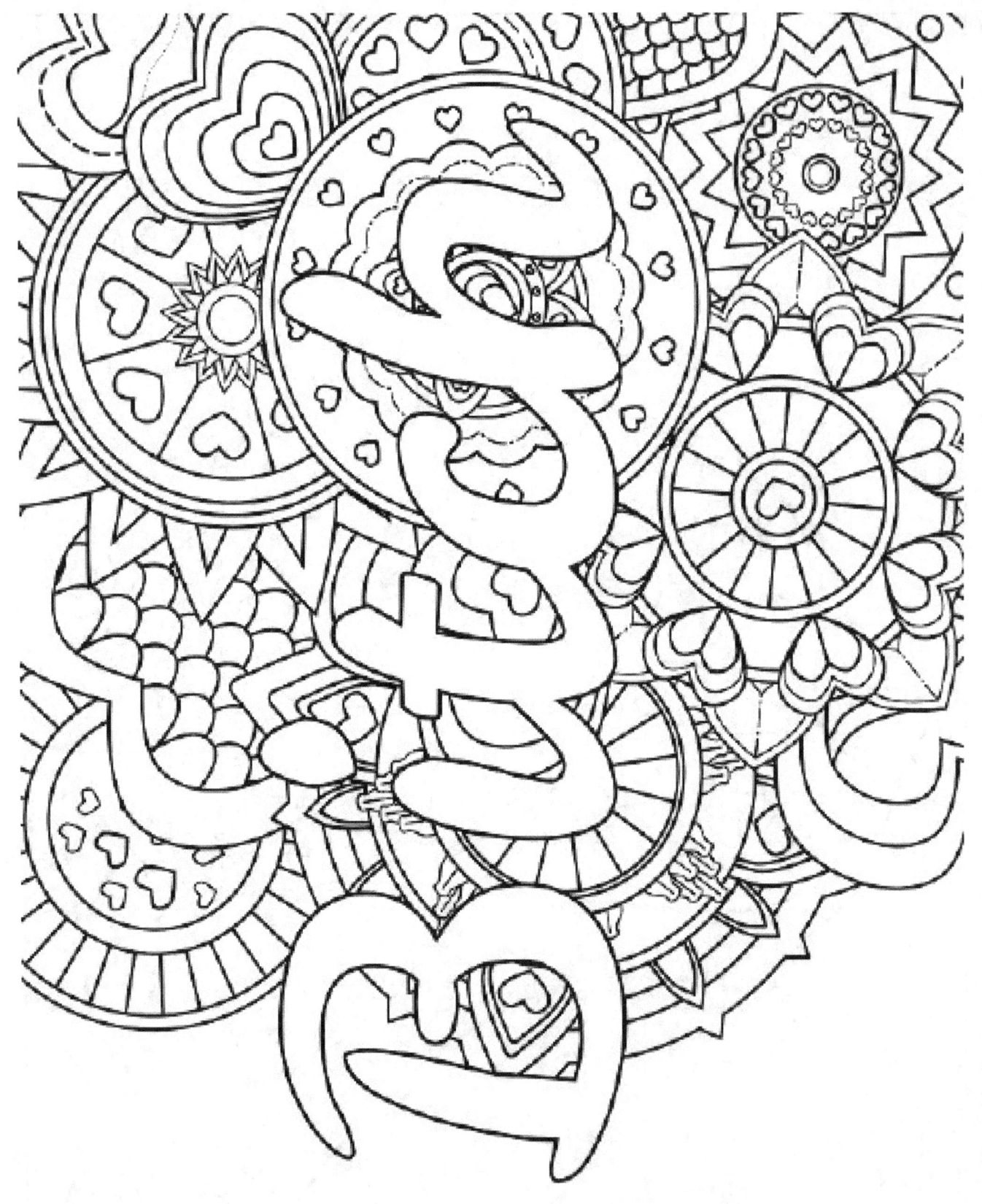

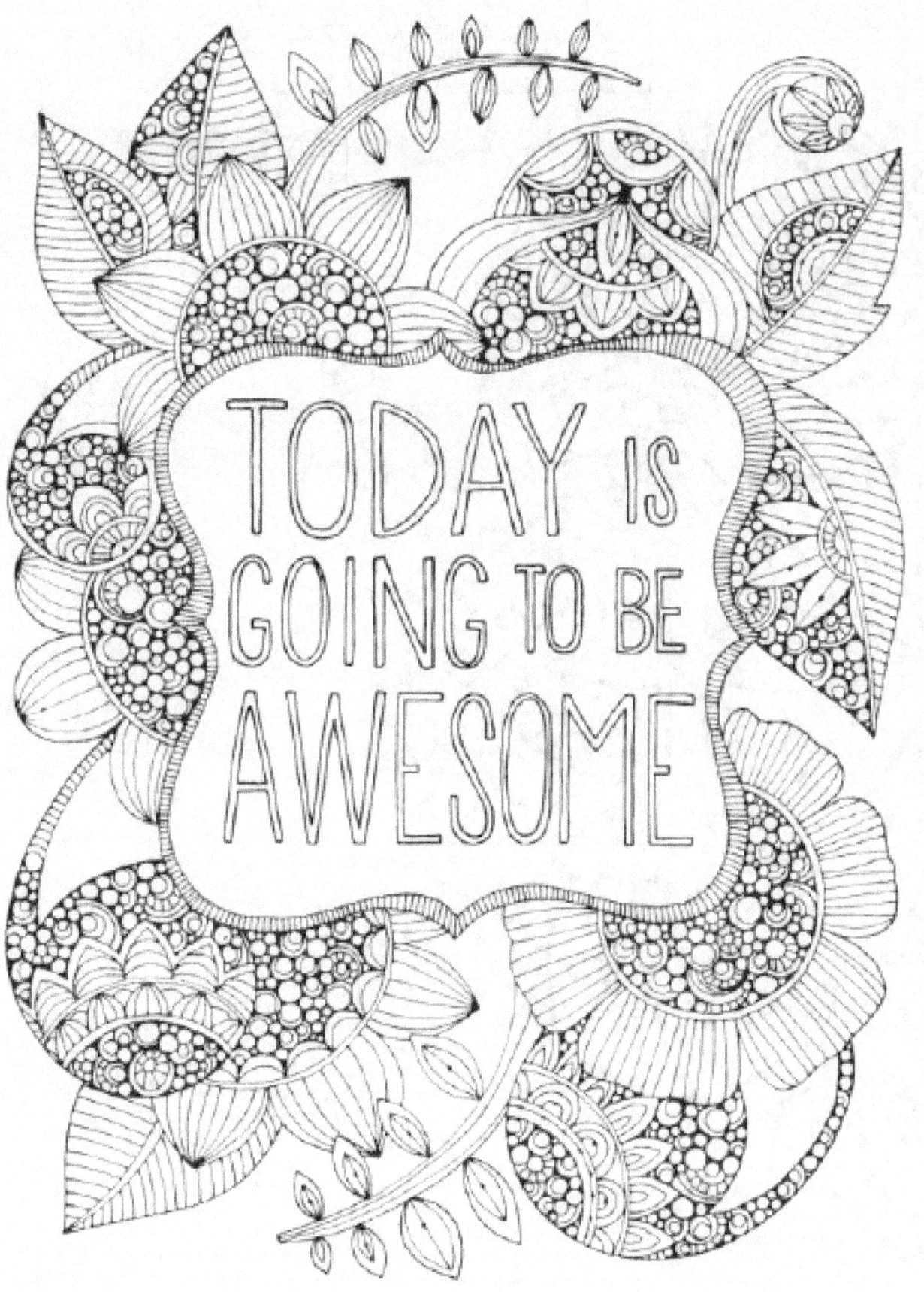

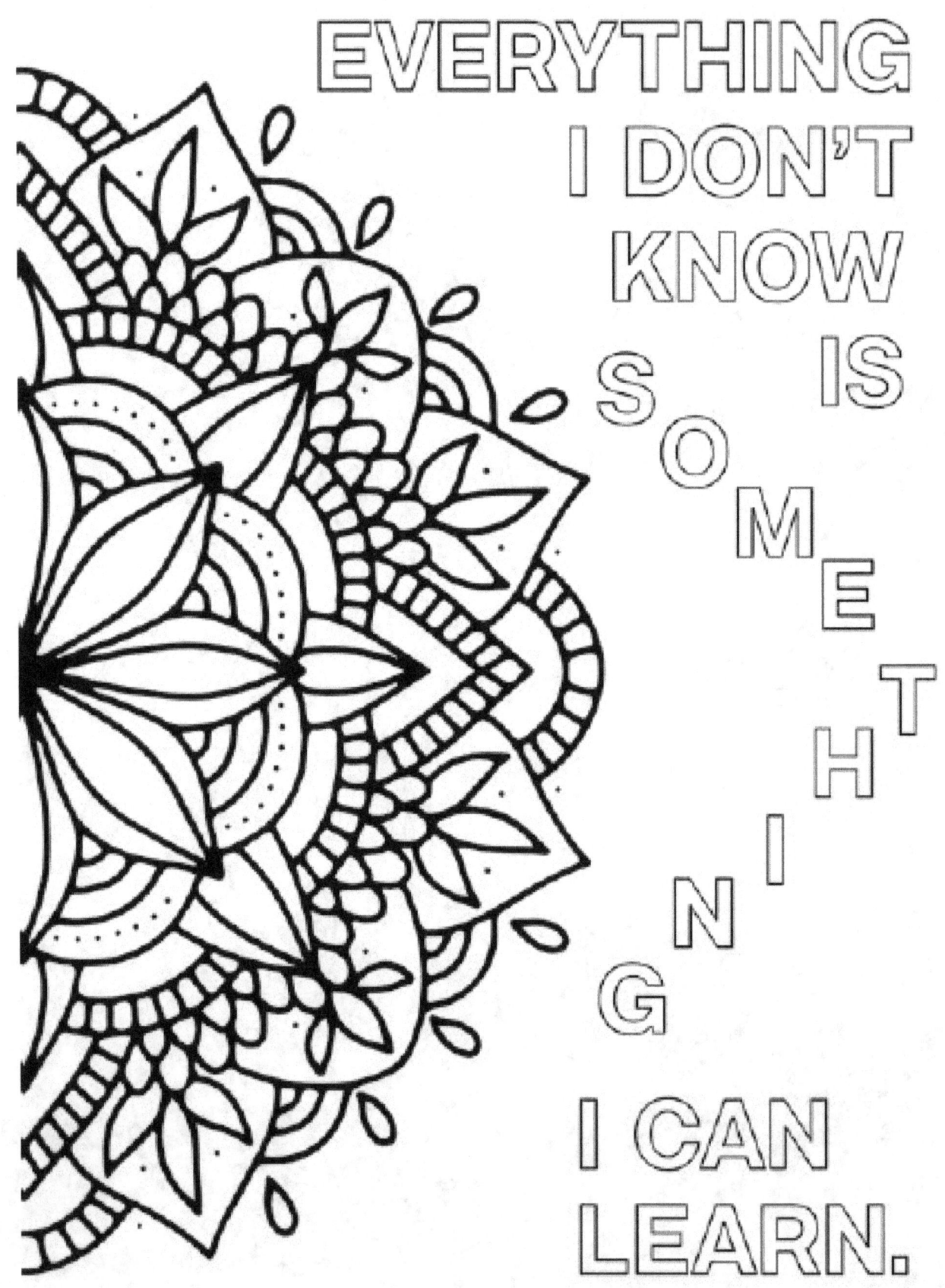

EVERYTHING I DON'T KNOW IS SOMETHING I CAN LEARN.

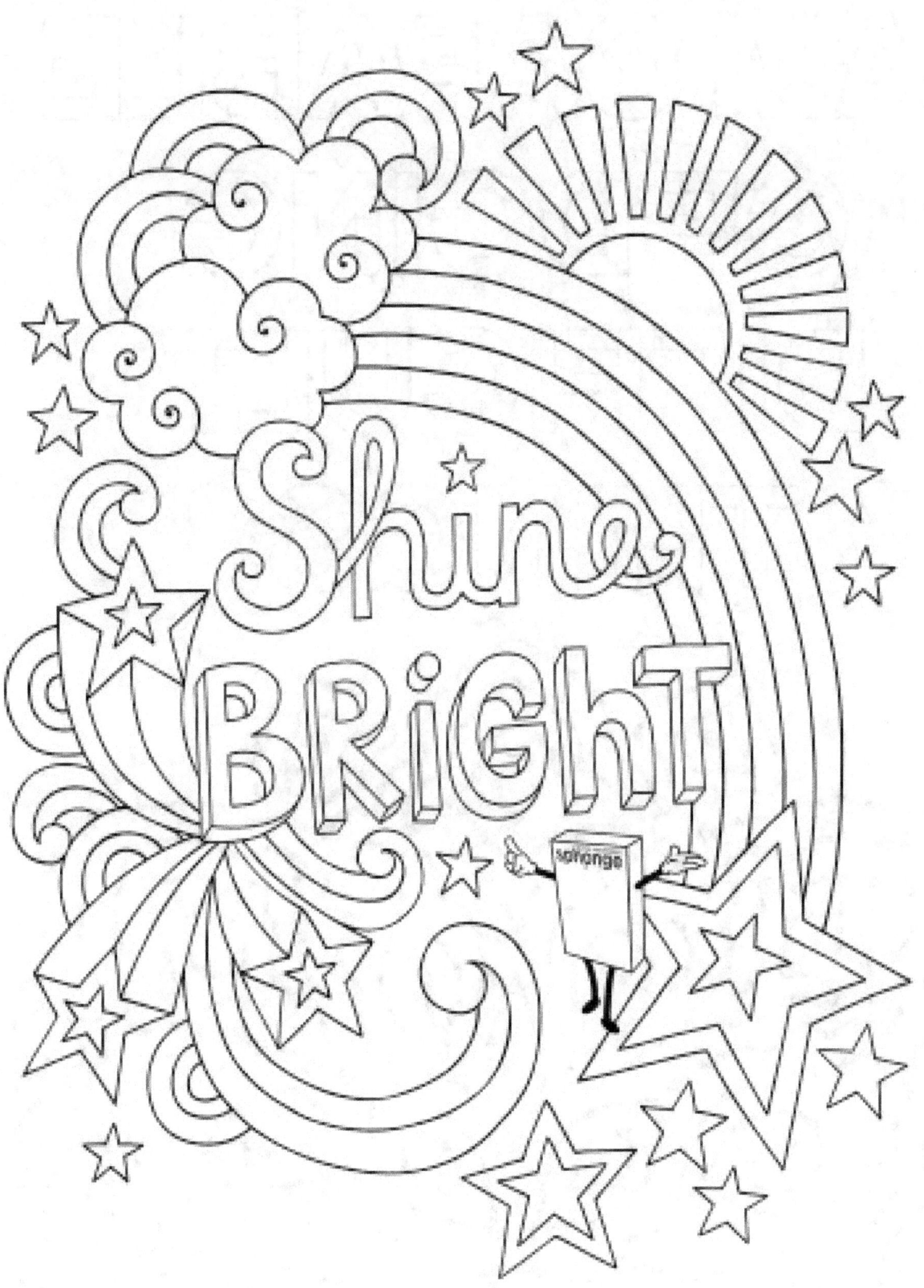

I AM CAPABLE OF DOING DIFFICULT THINGS.

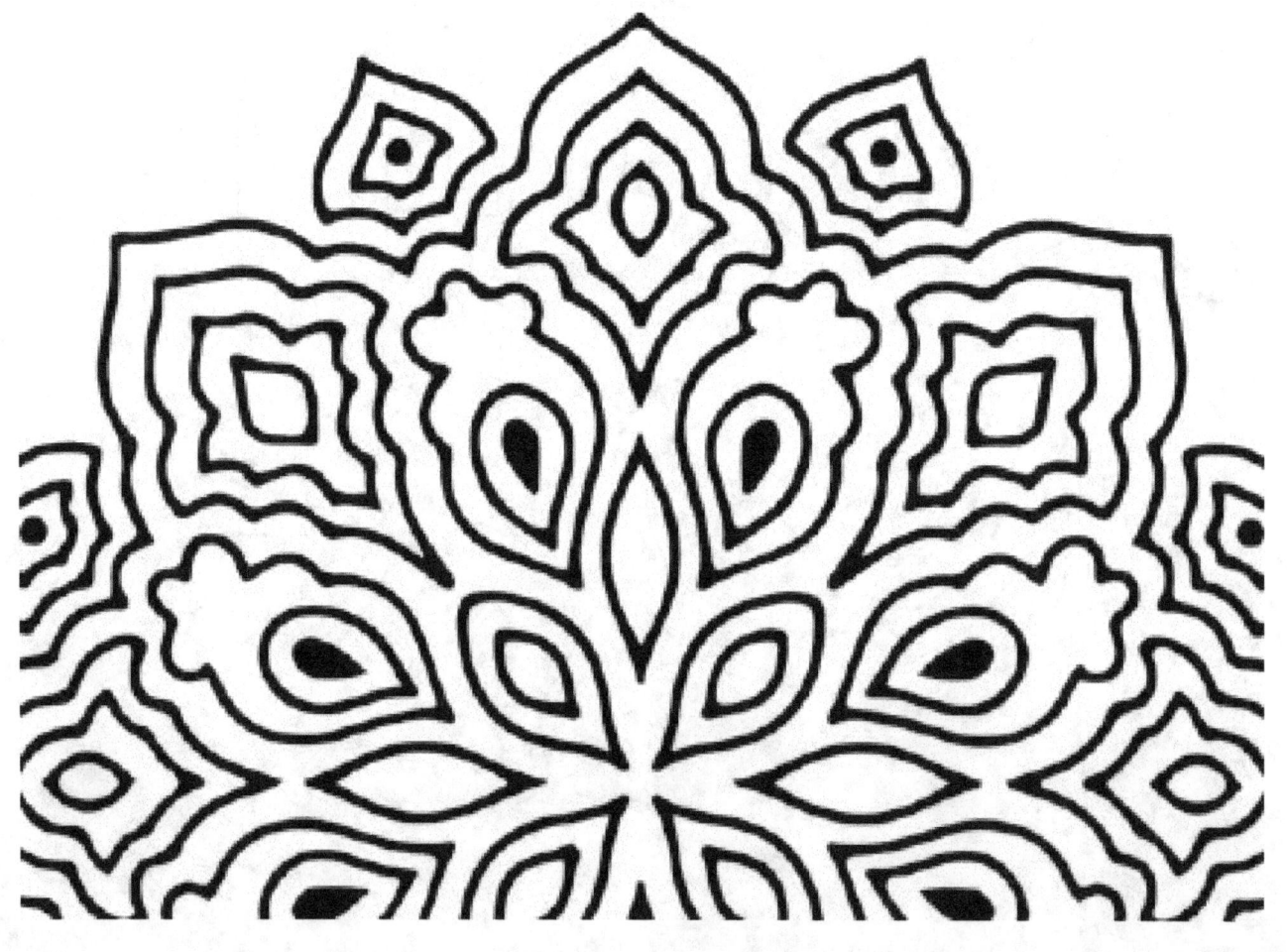

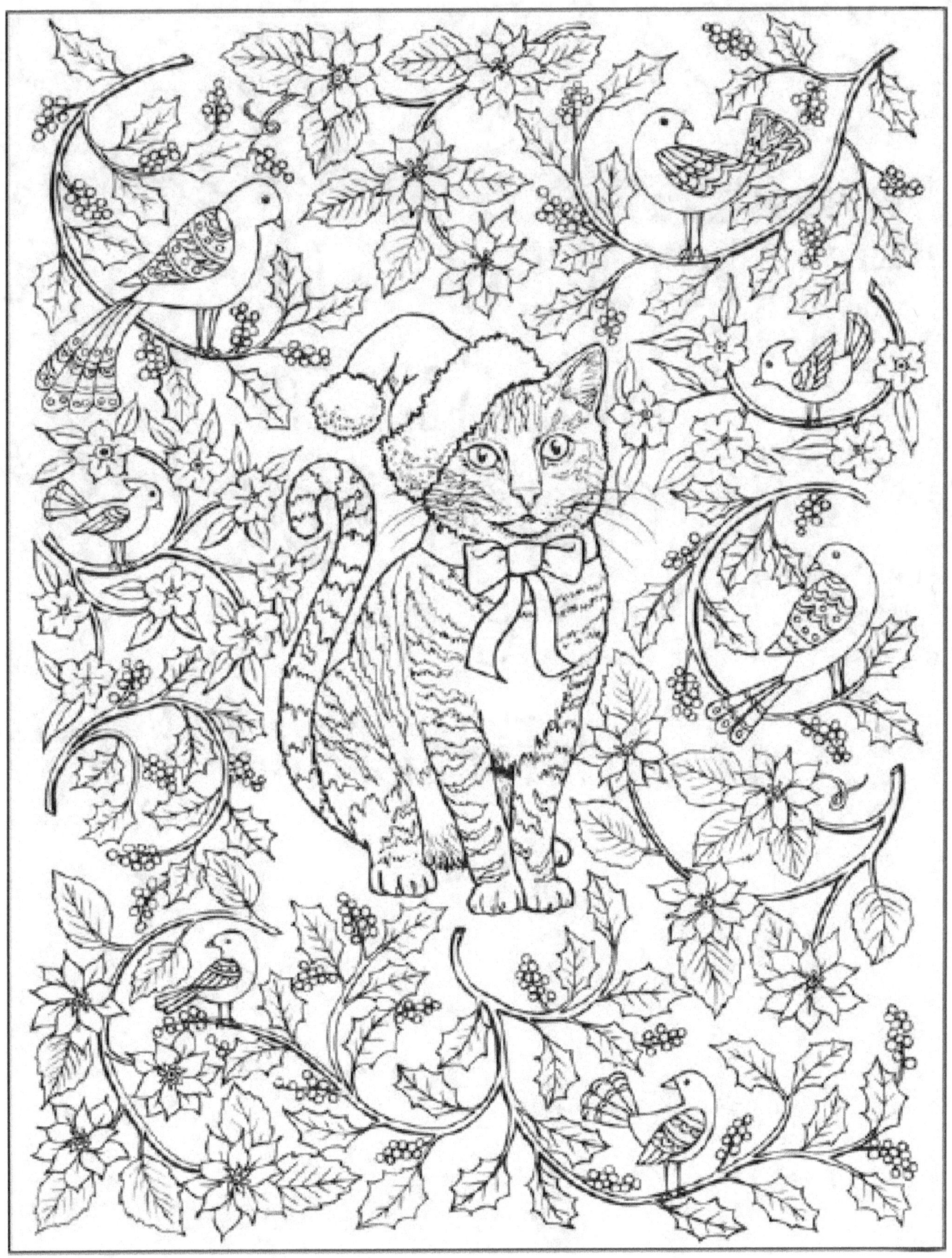

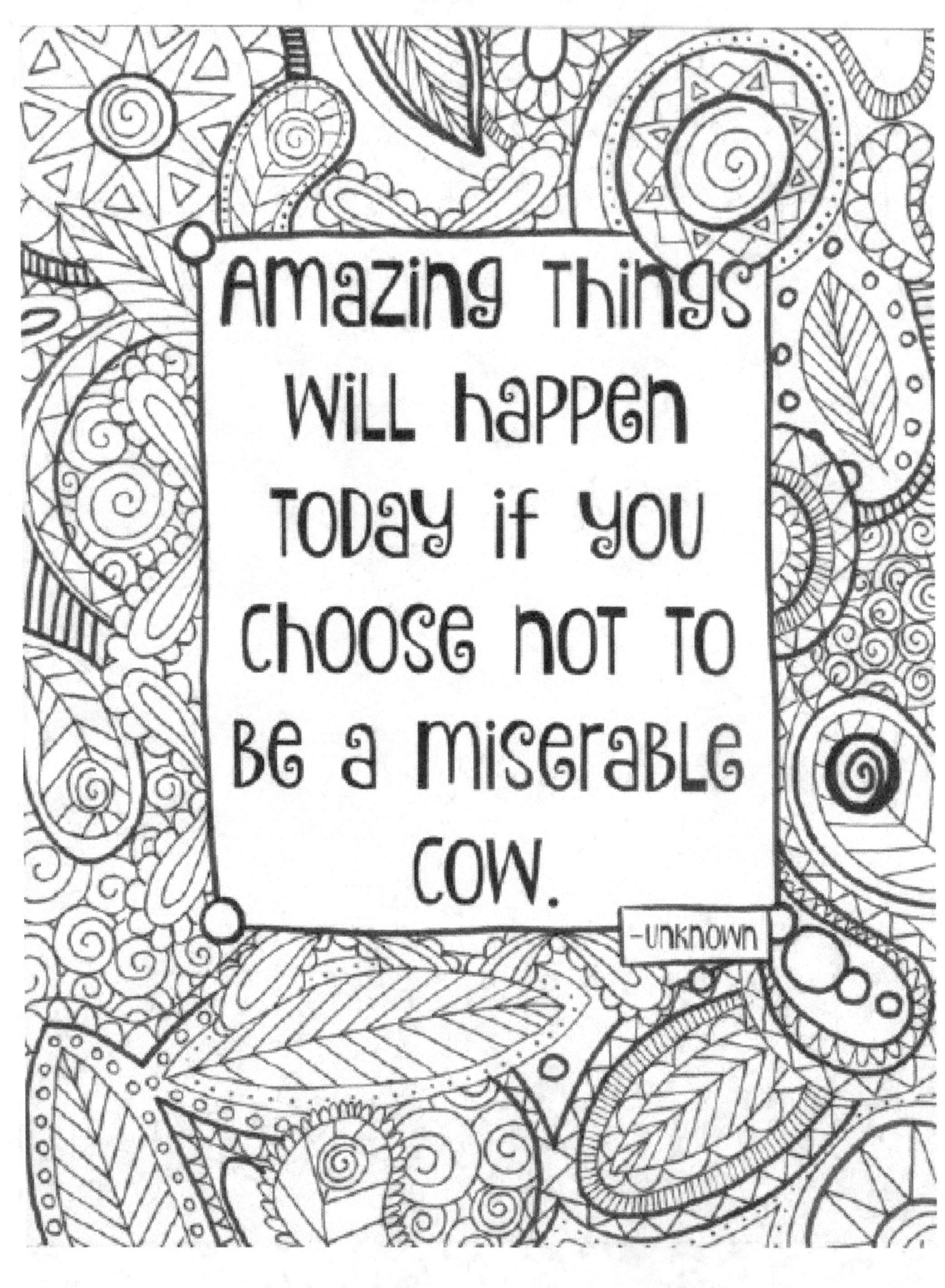

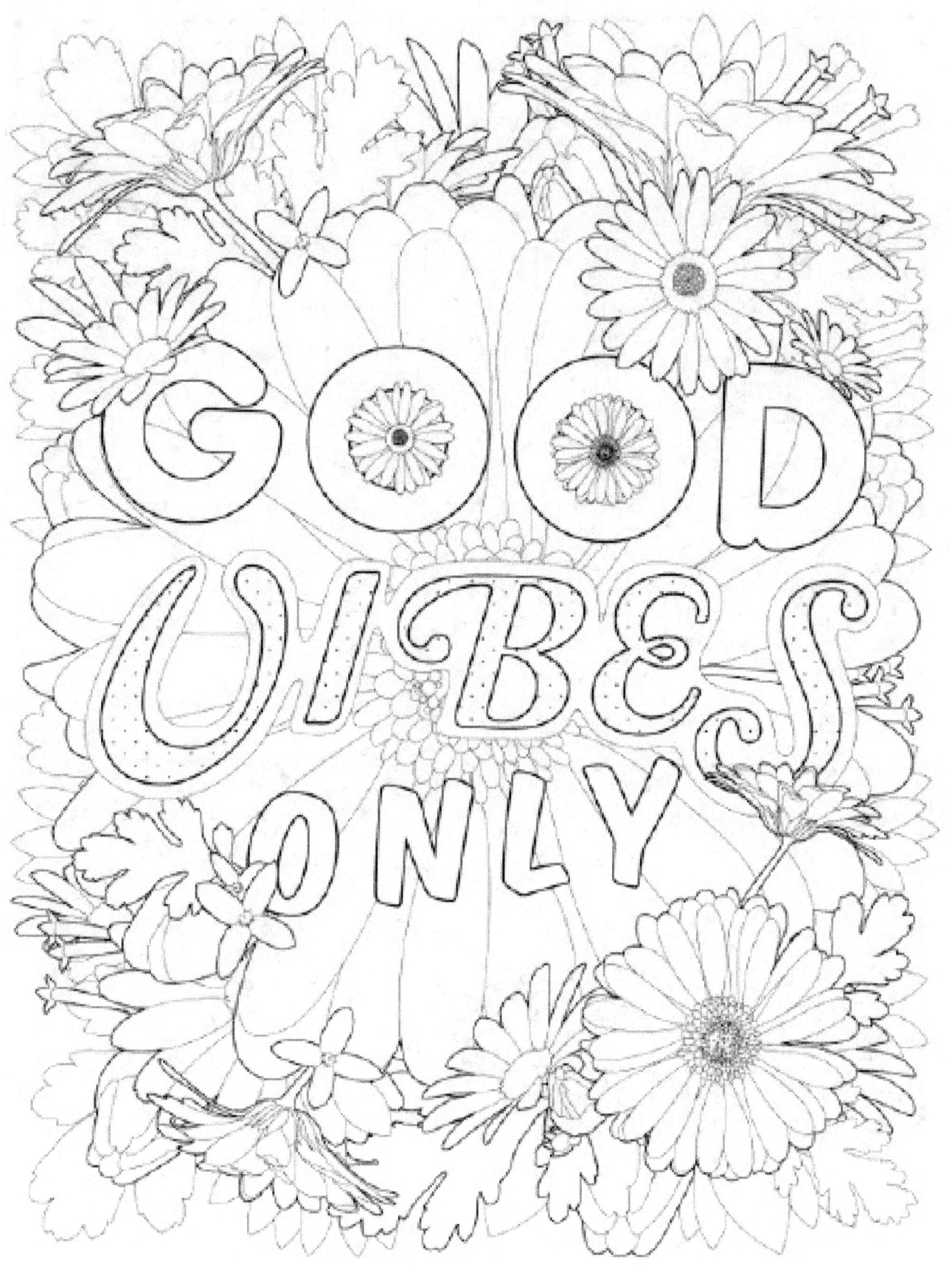

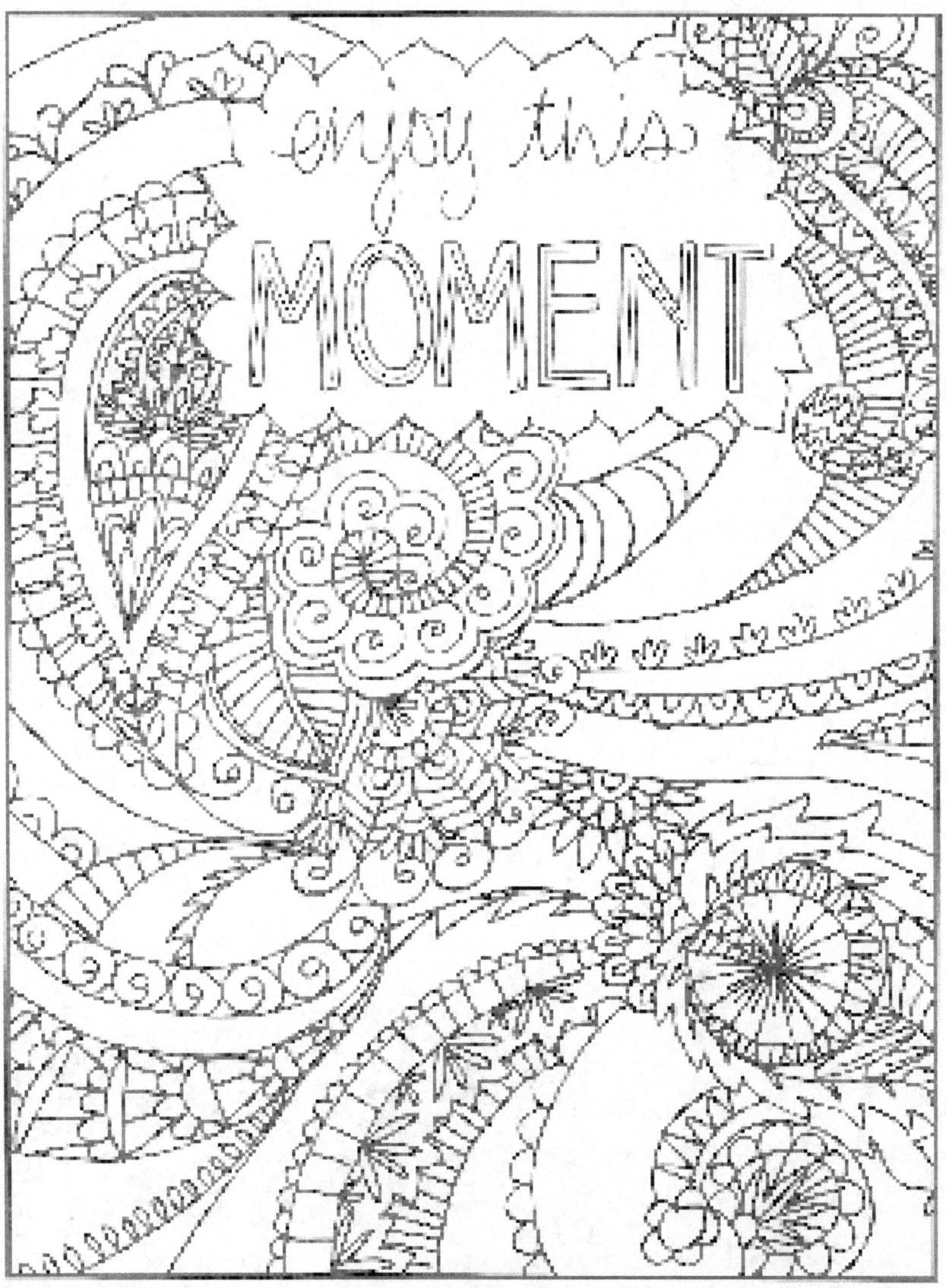

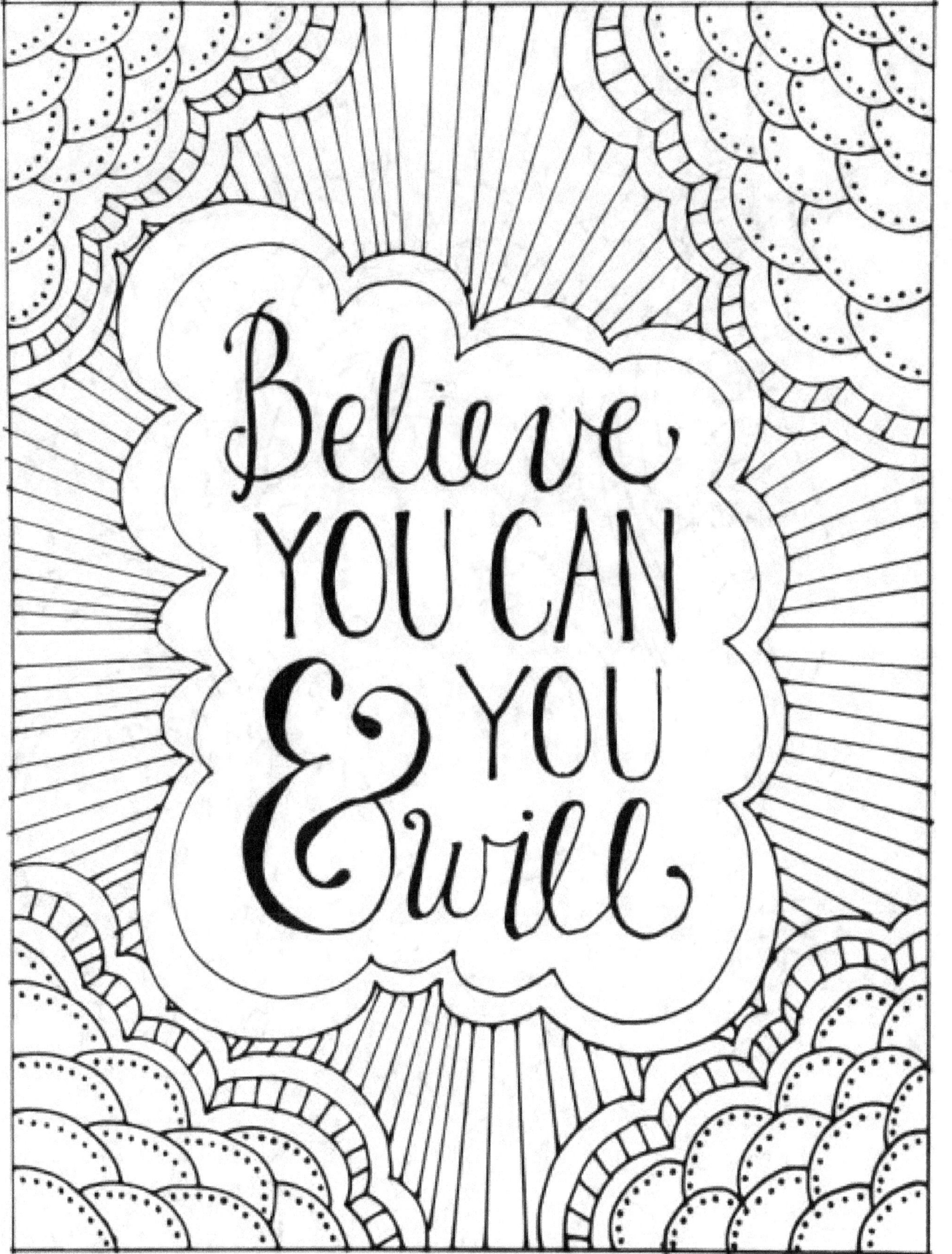

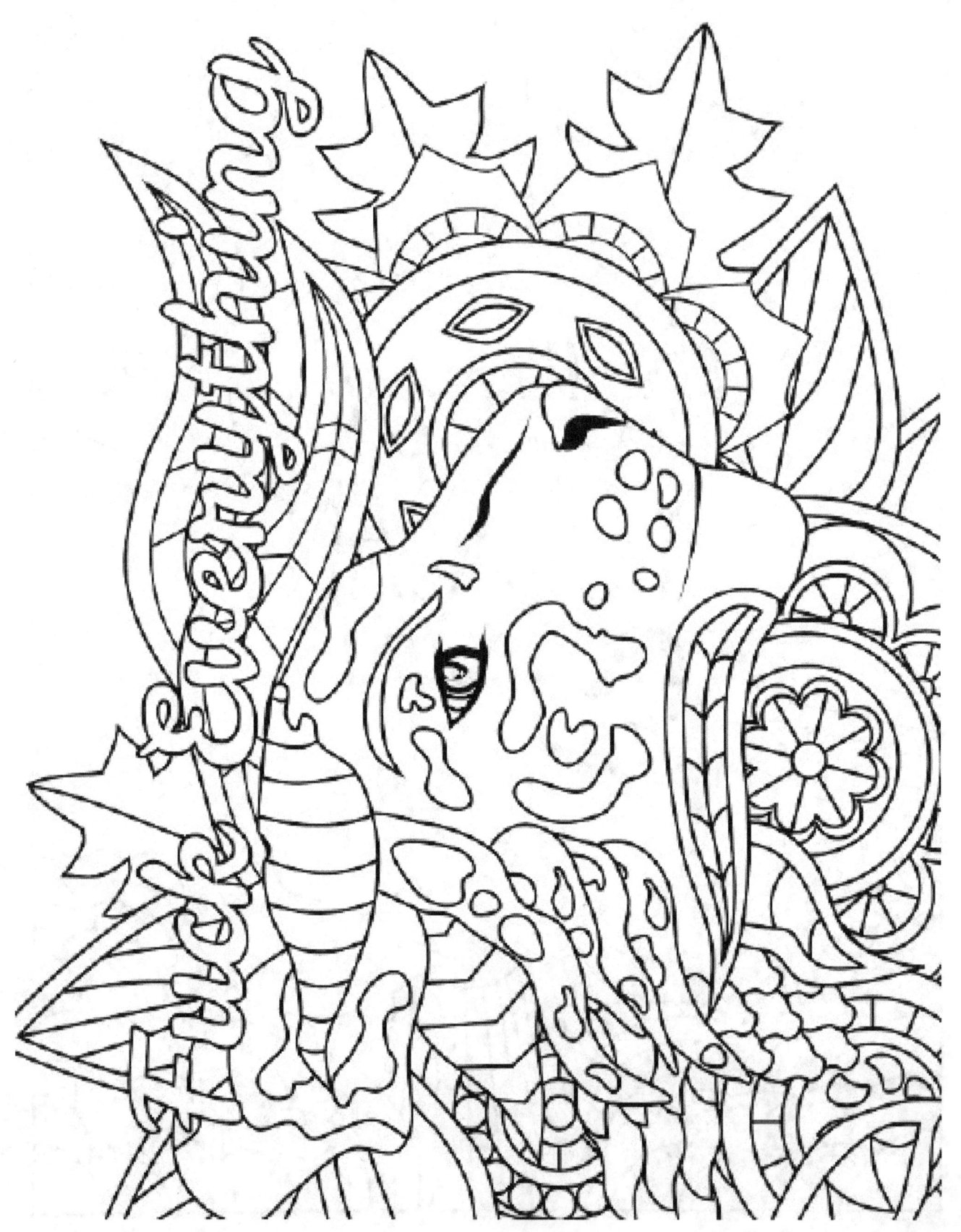

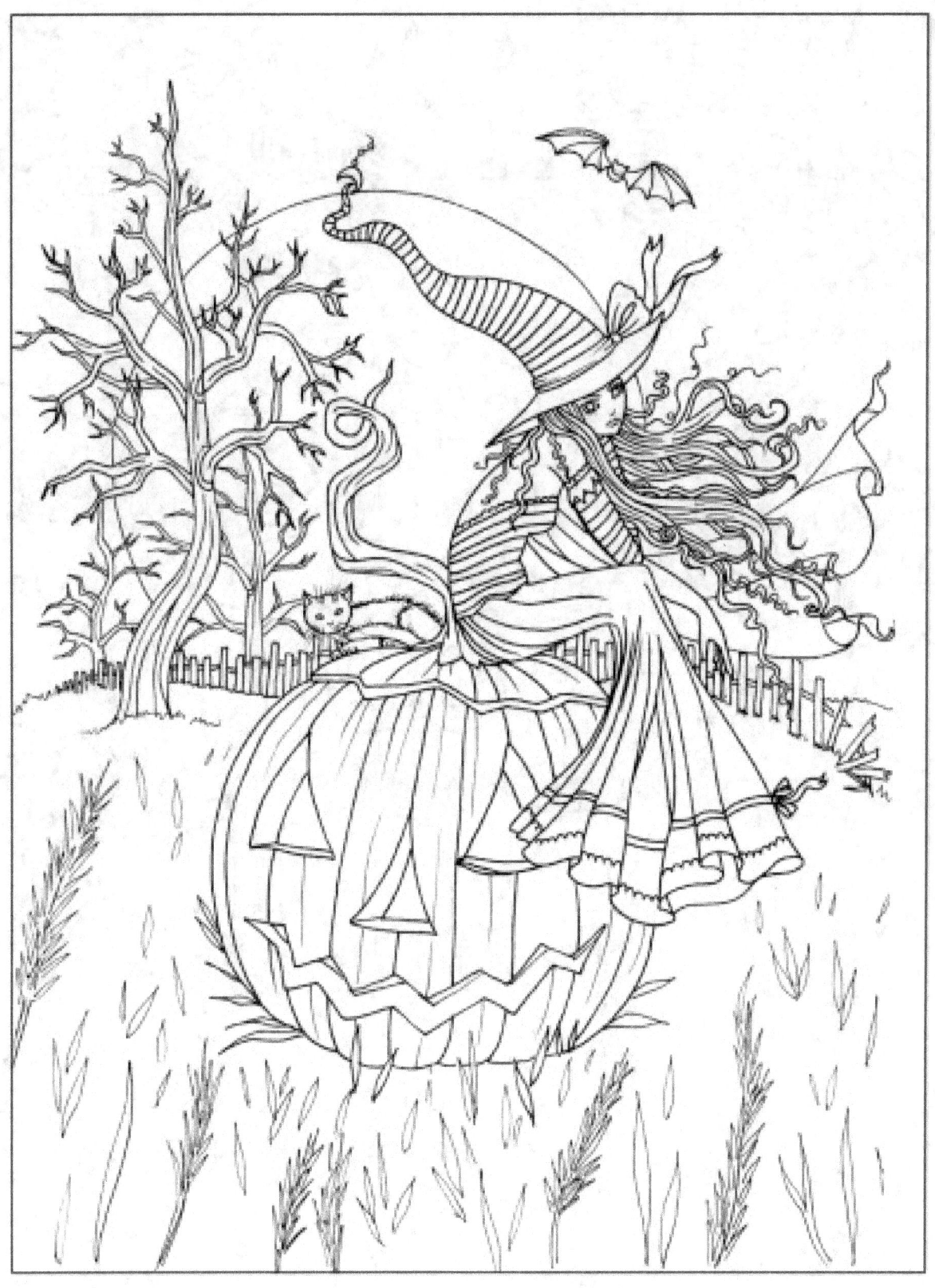

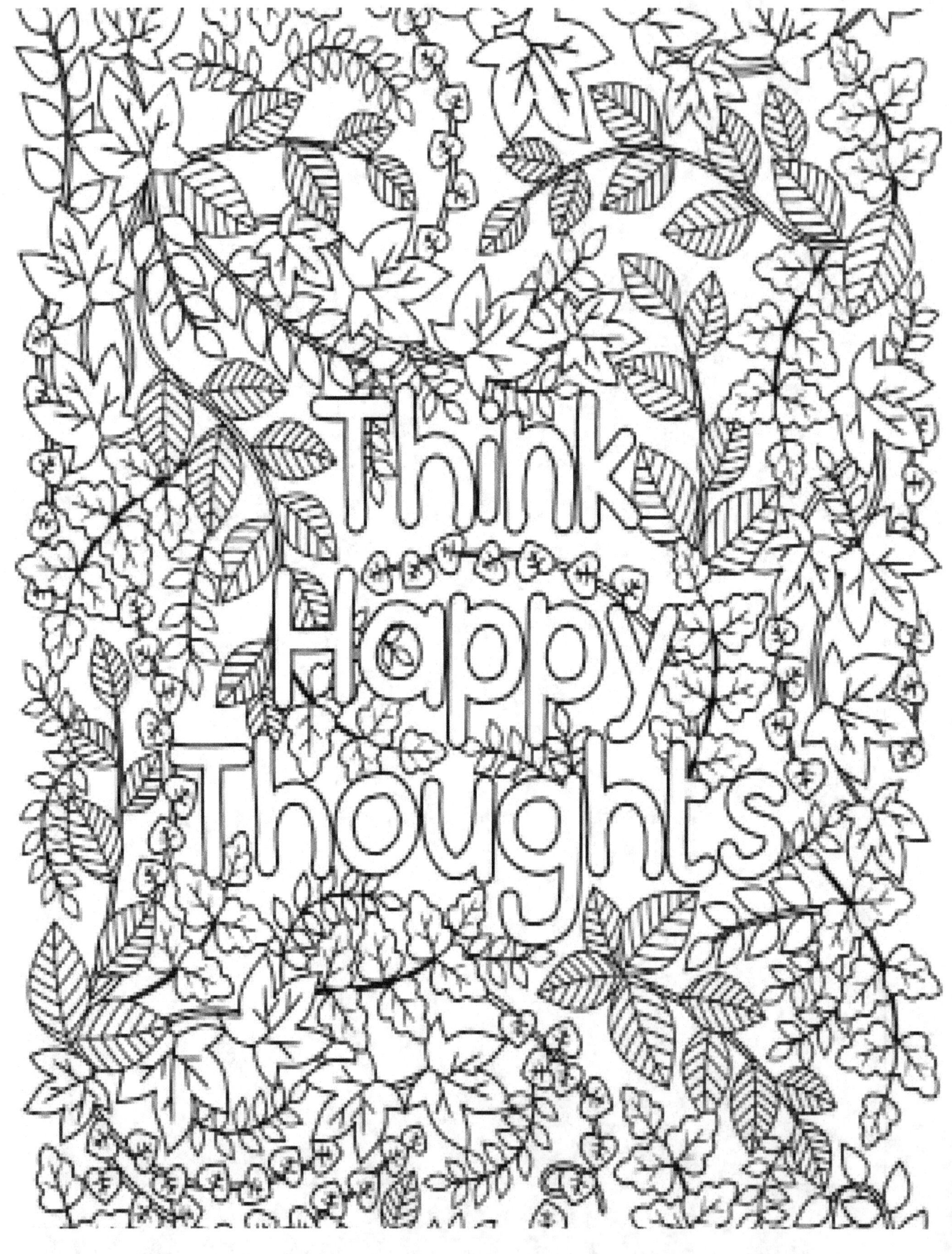

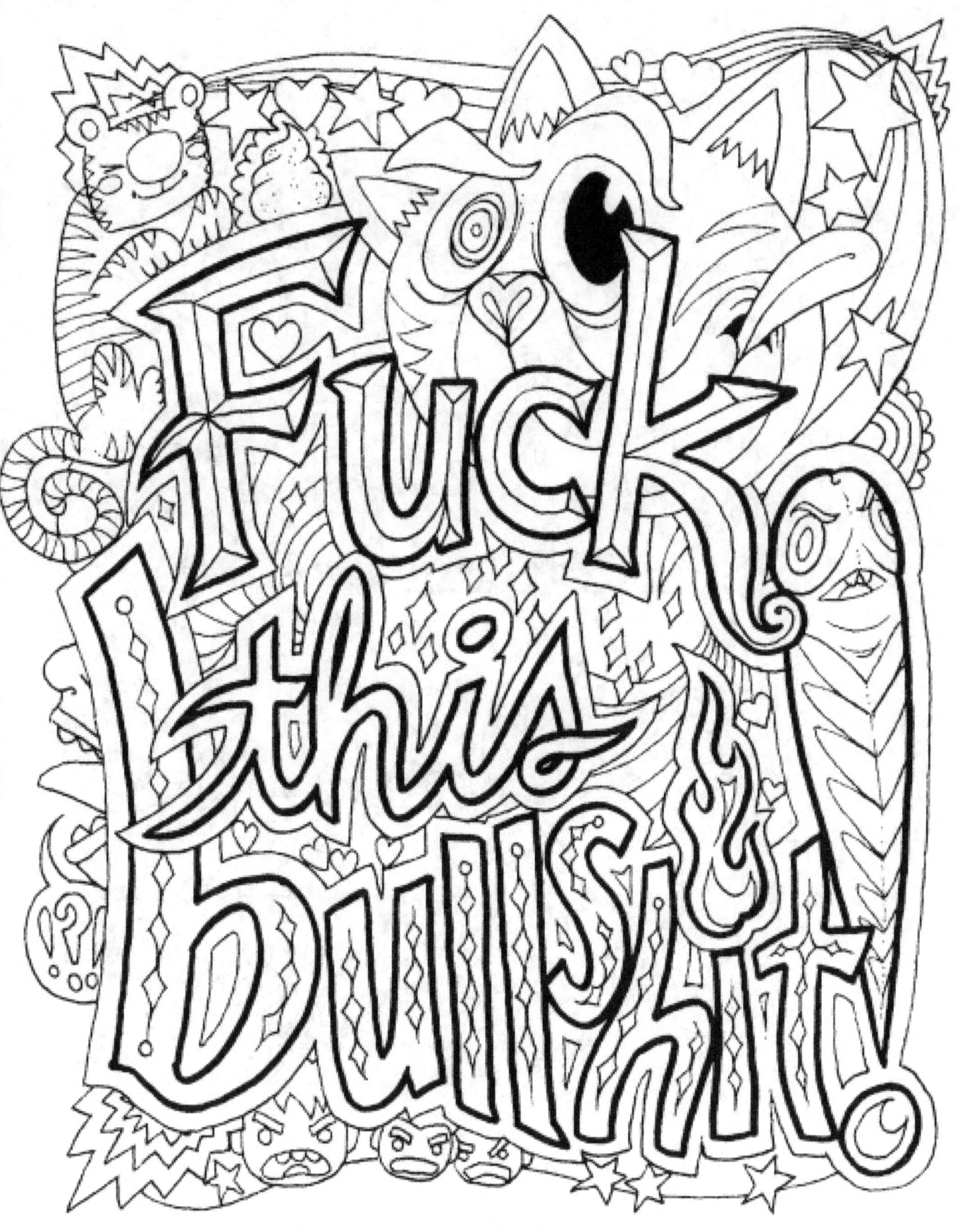

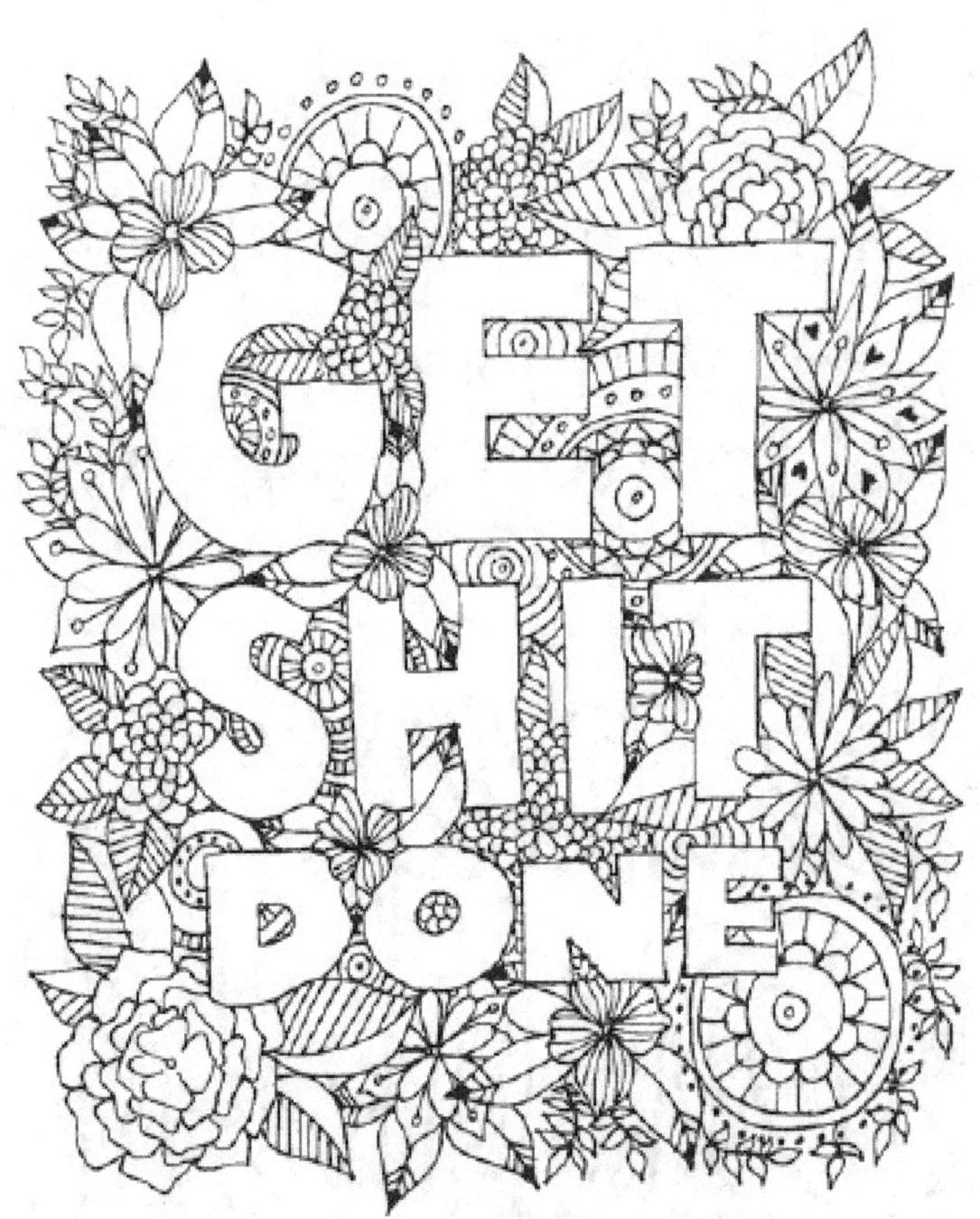

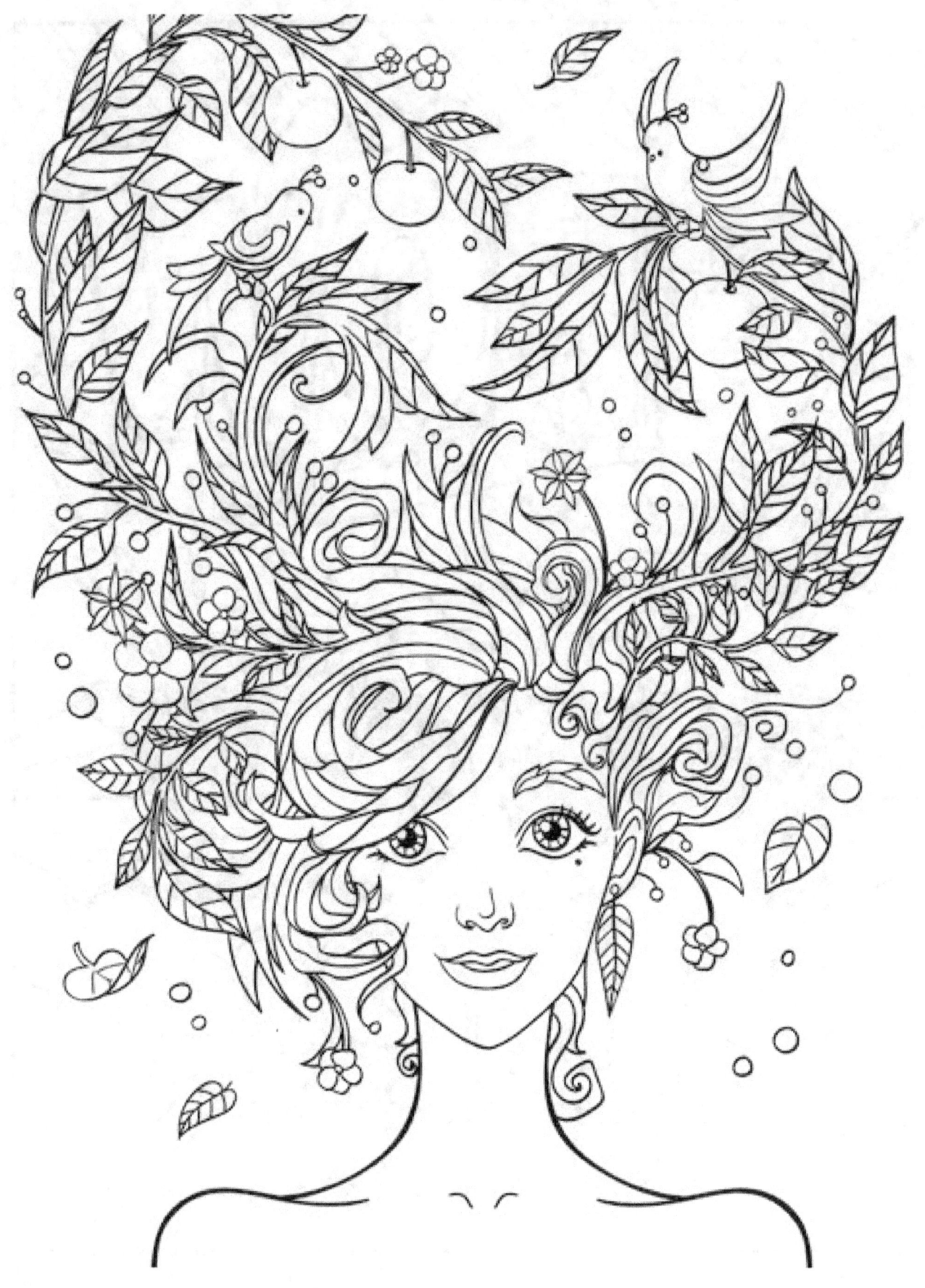

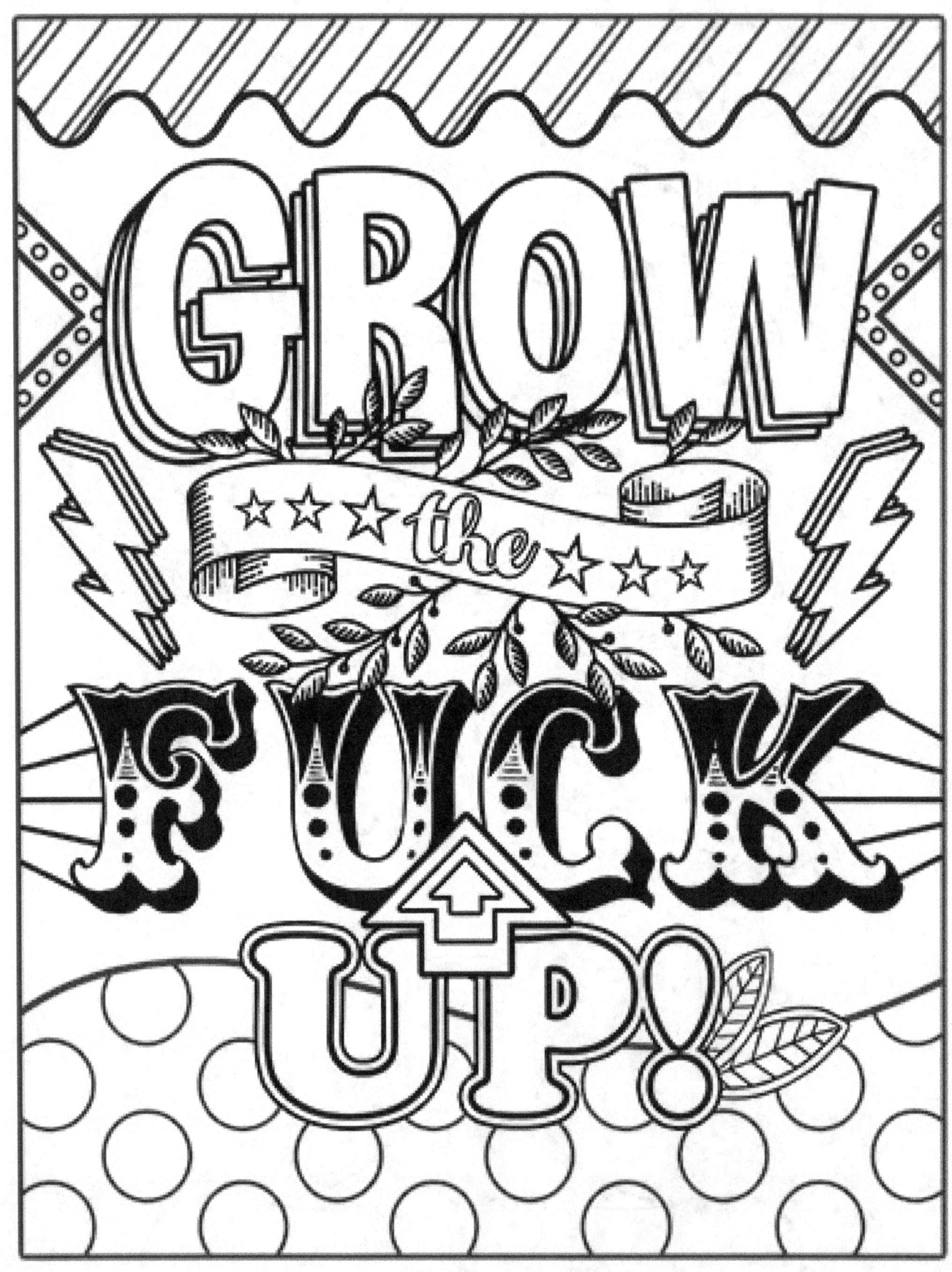

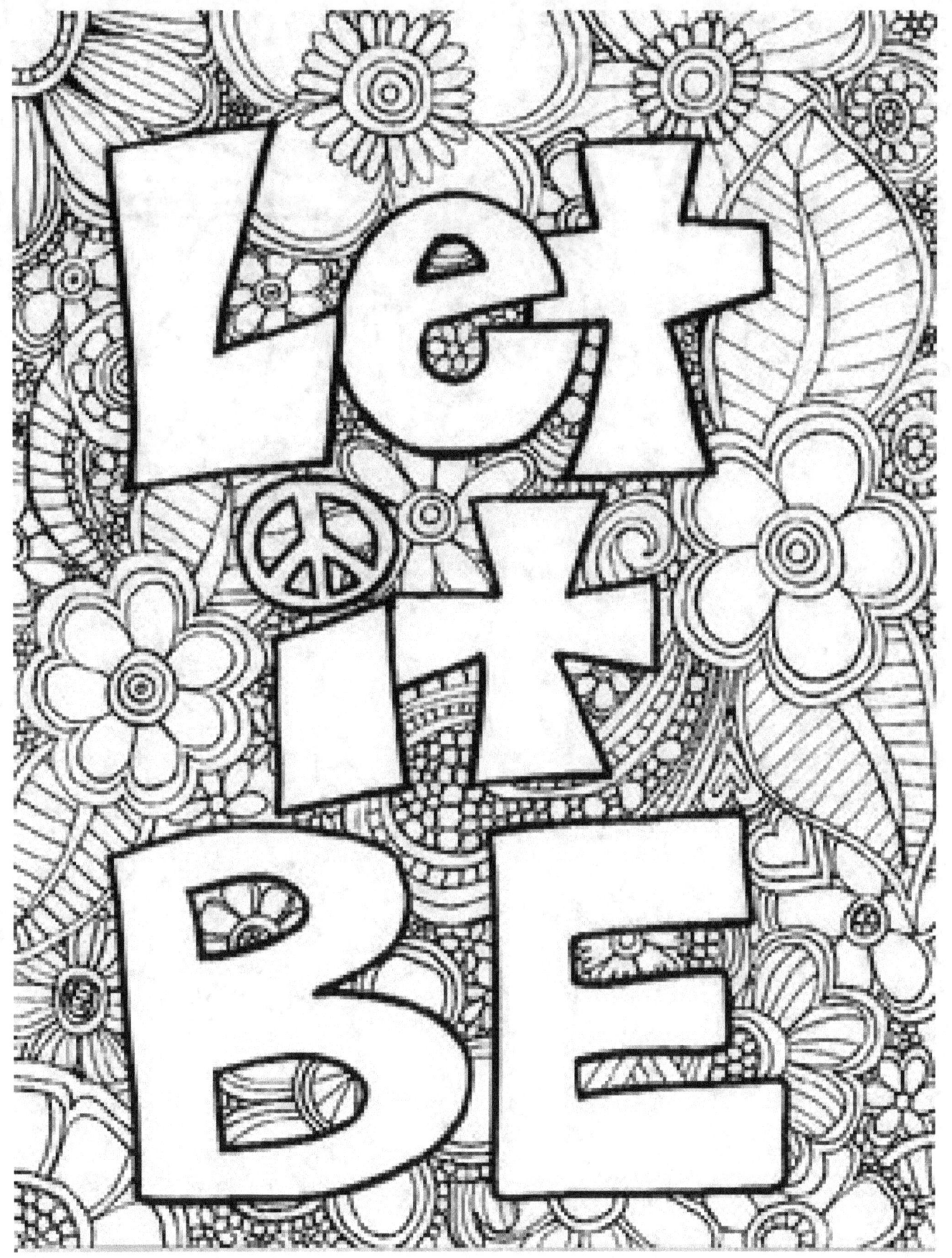

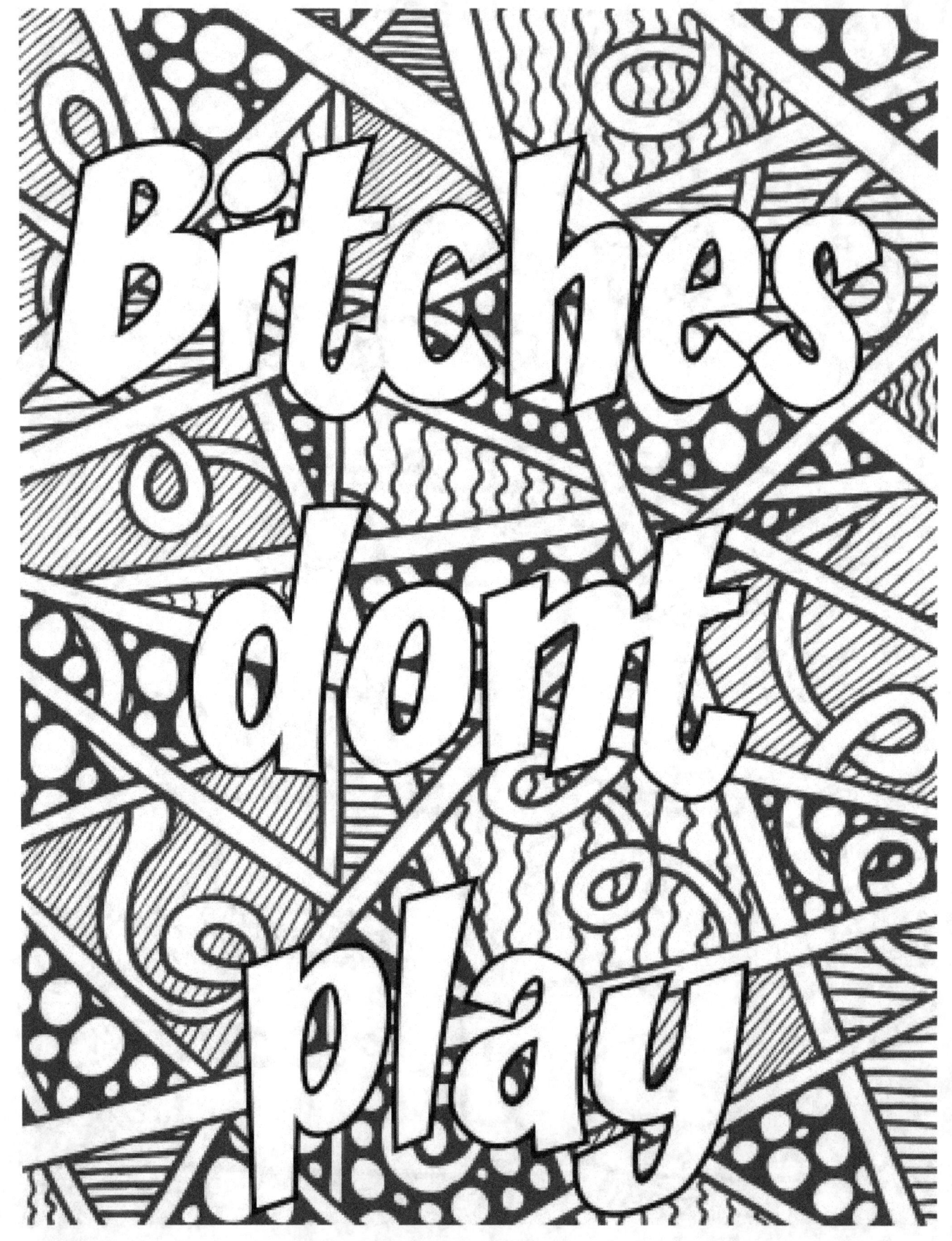

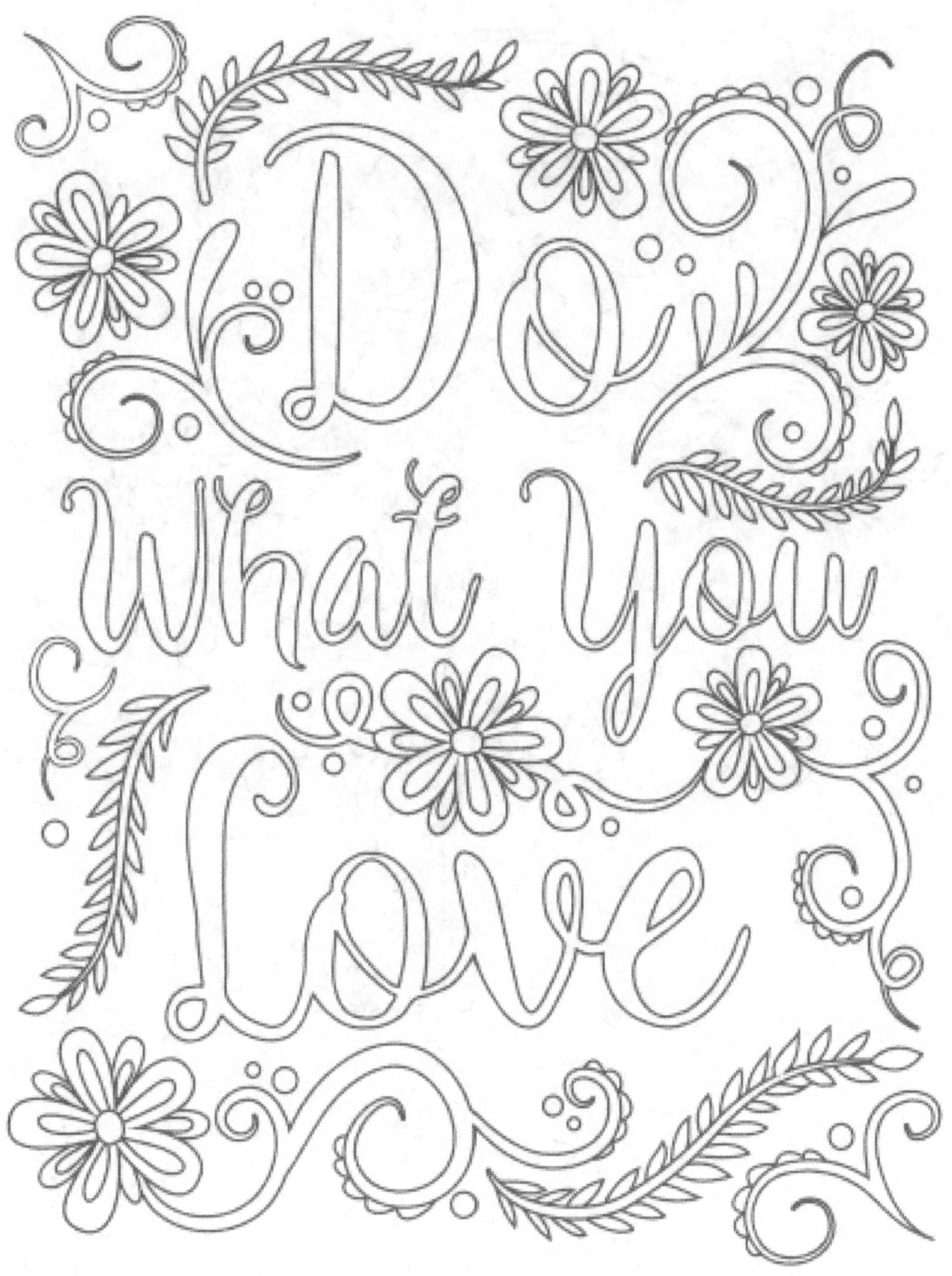

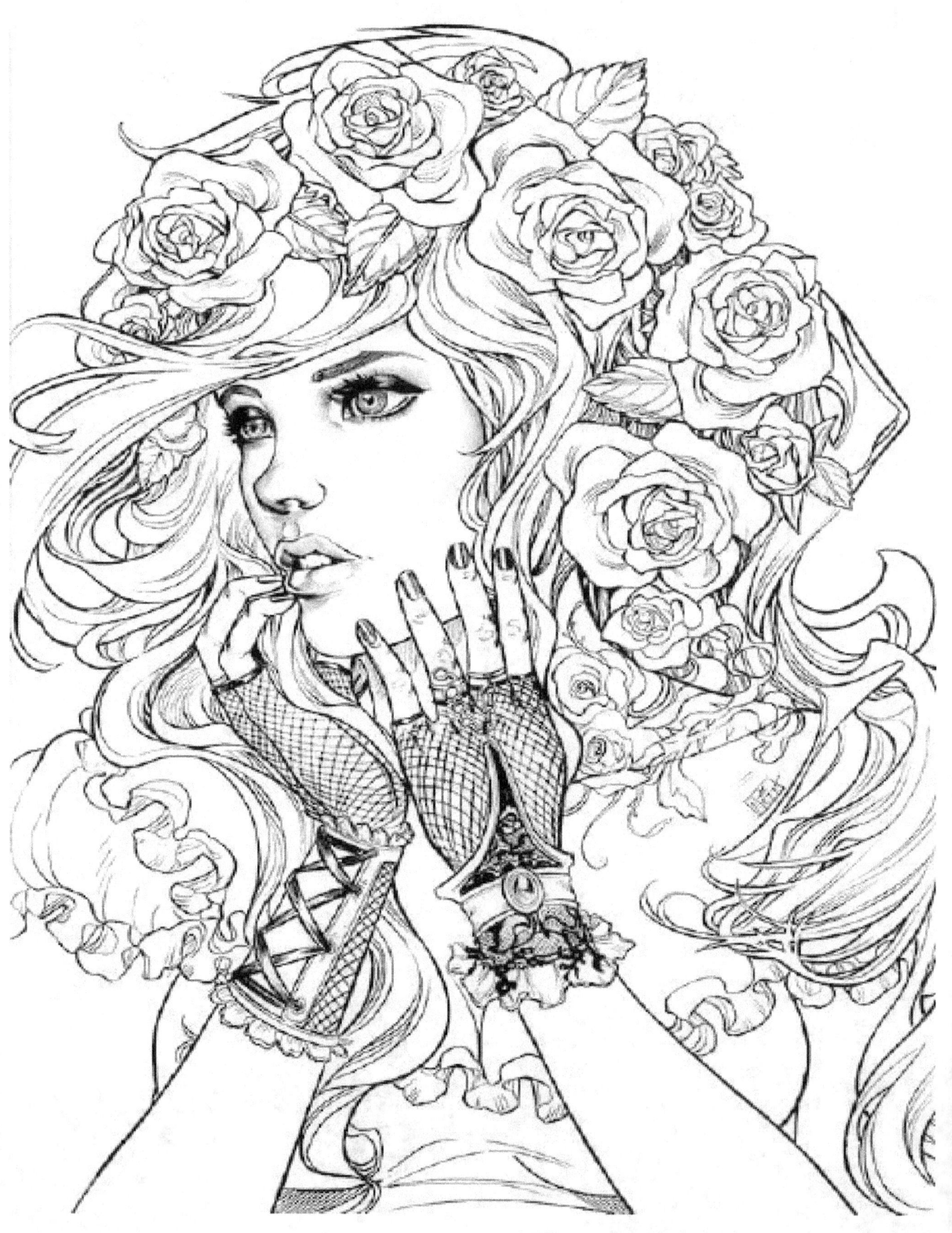

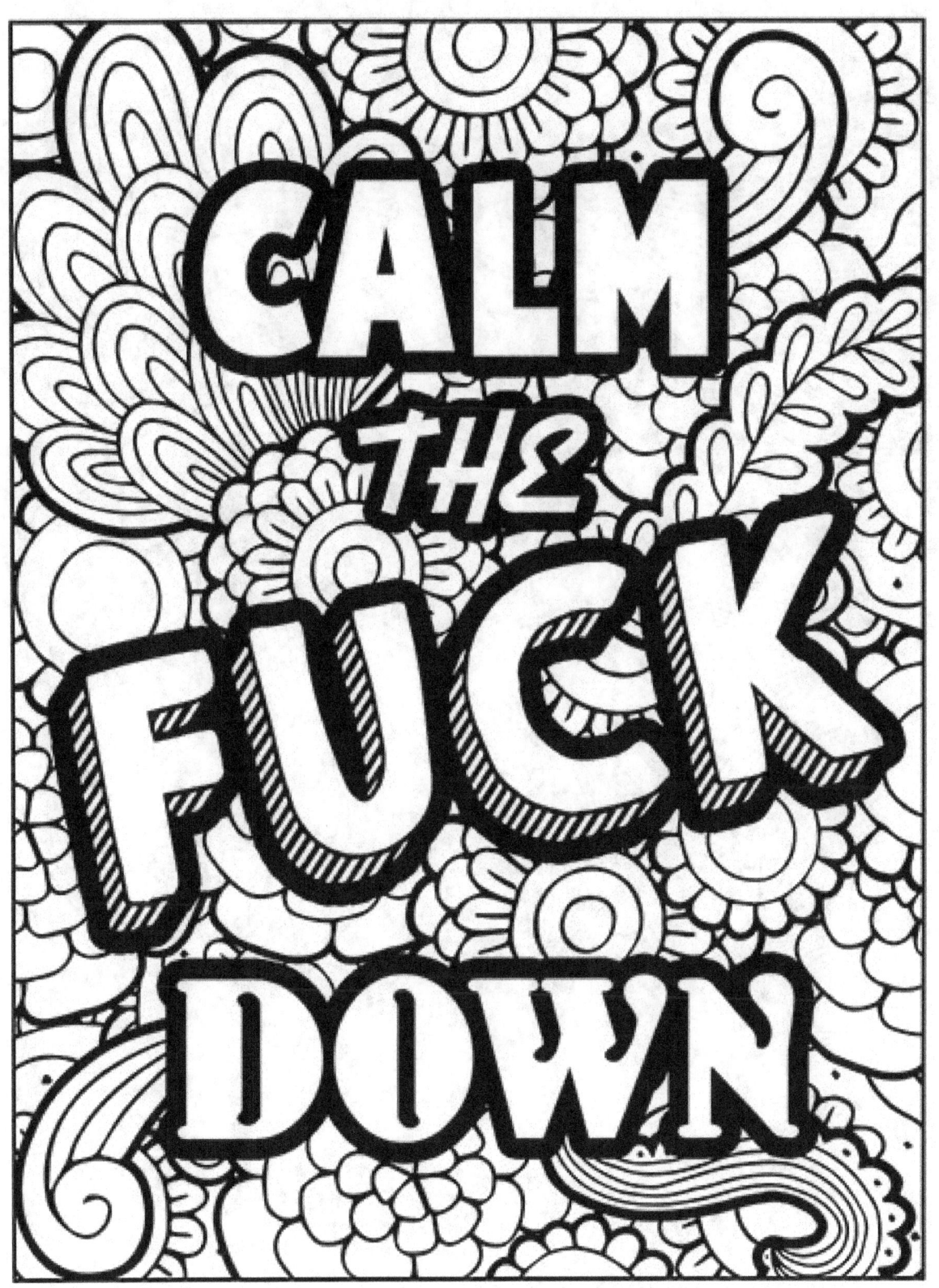

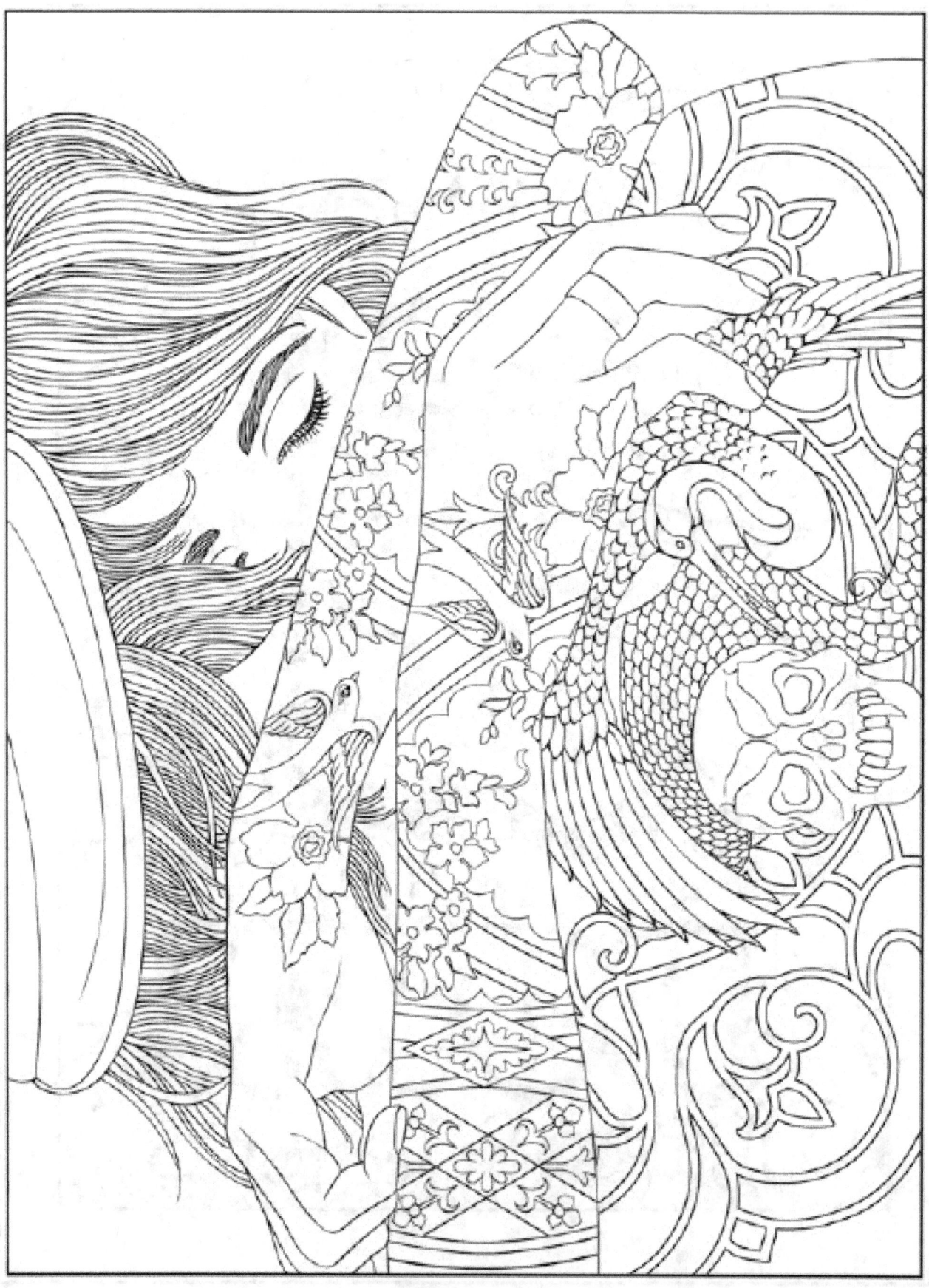

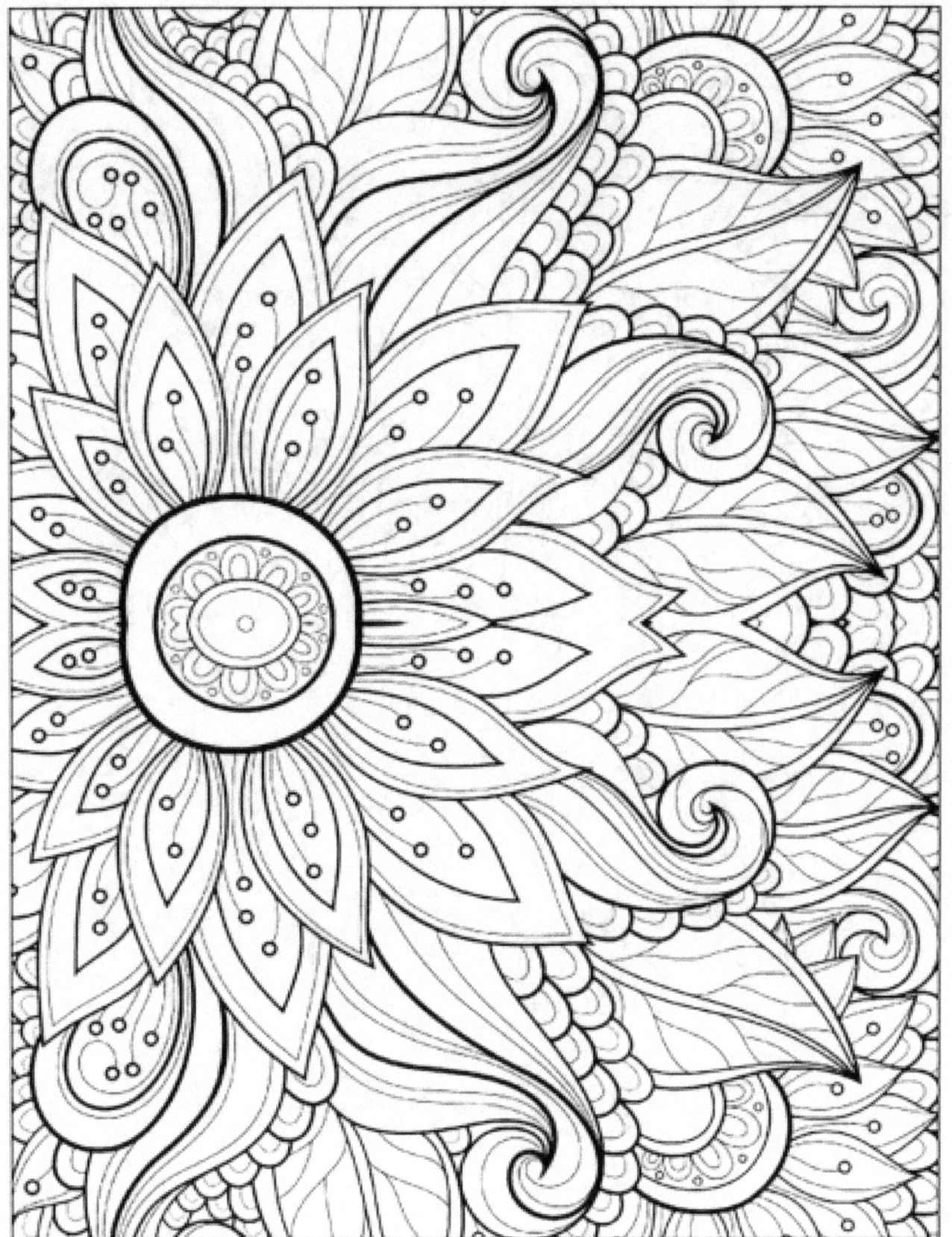

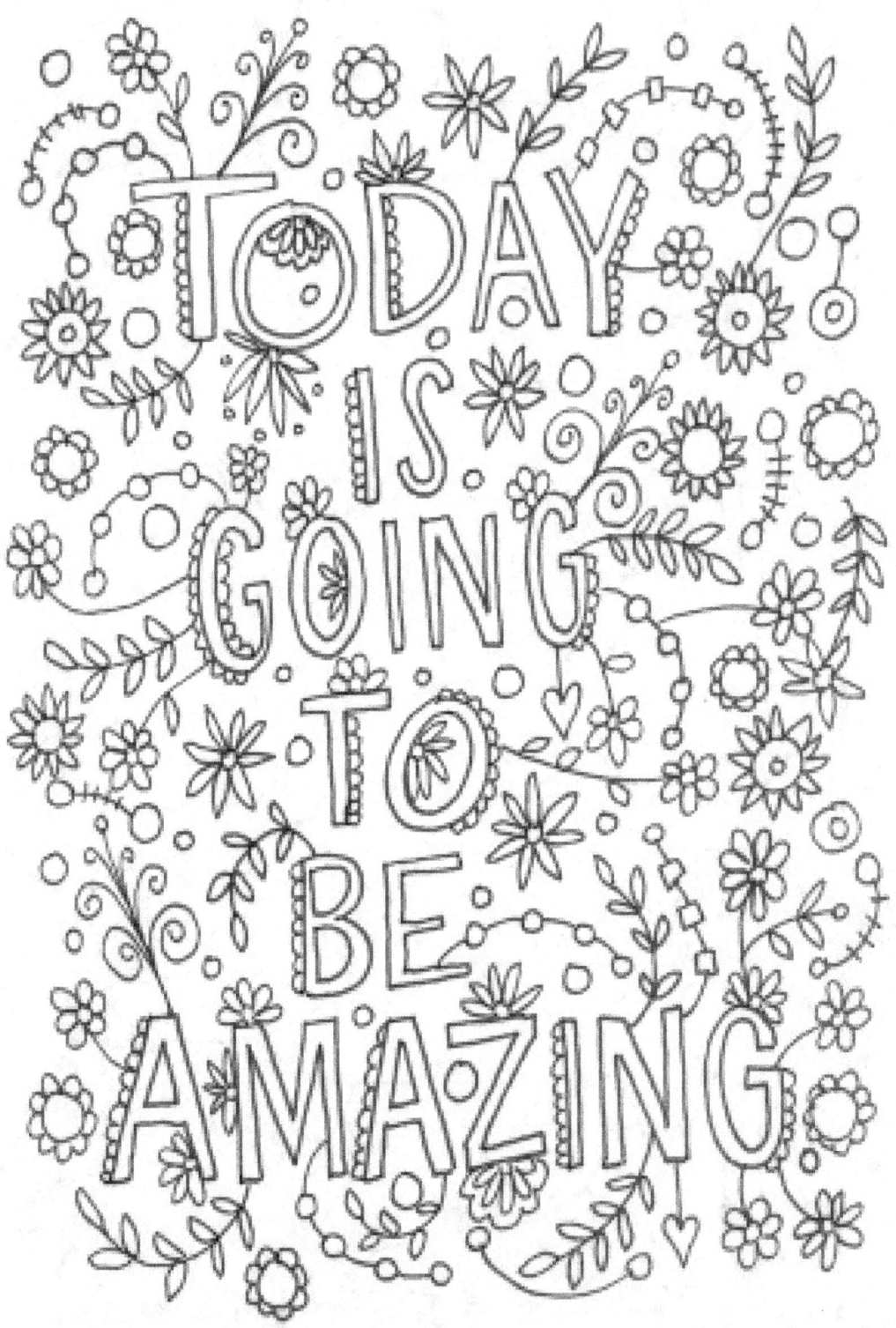

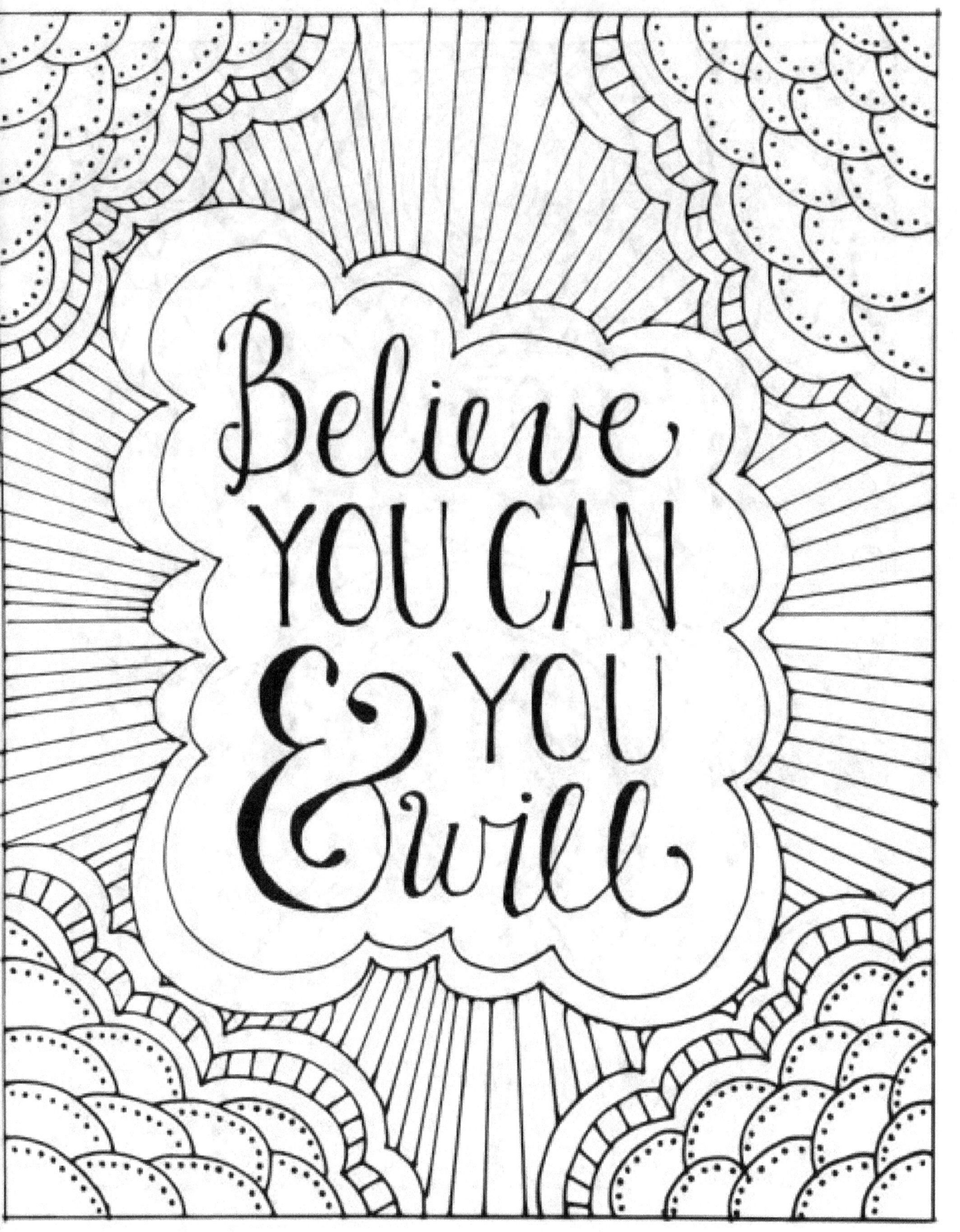

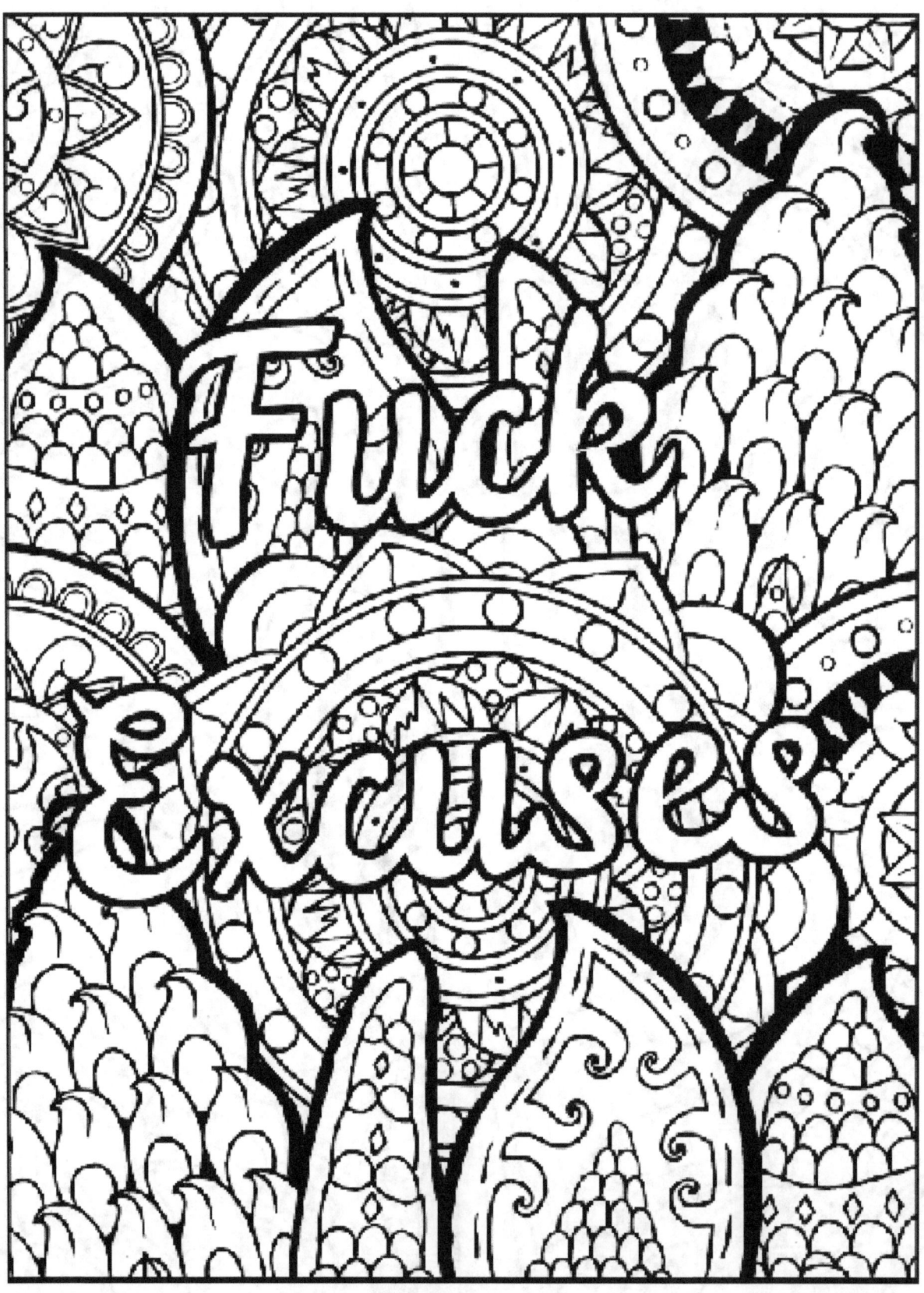

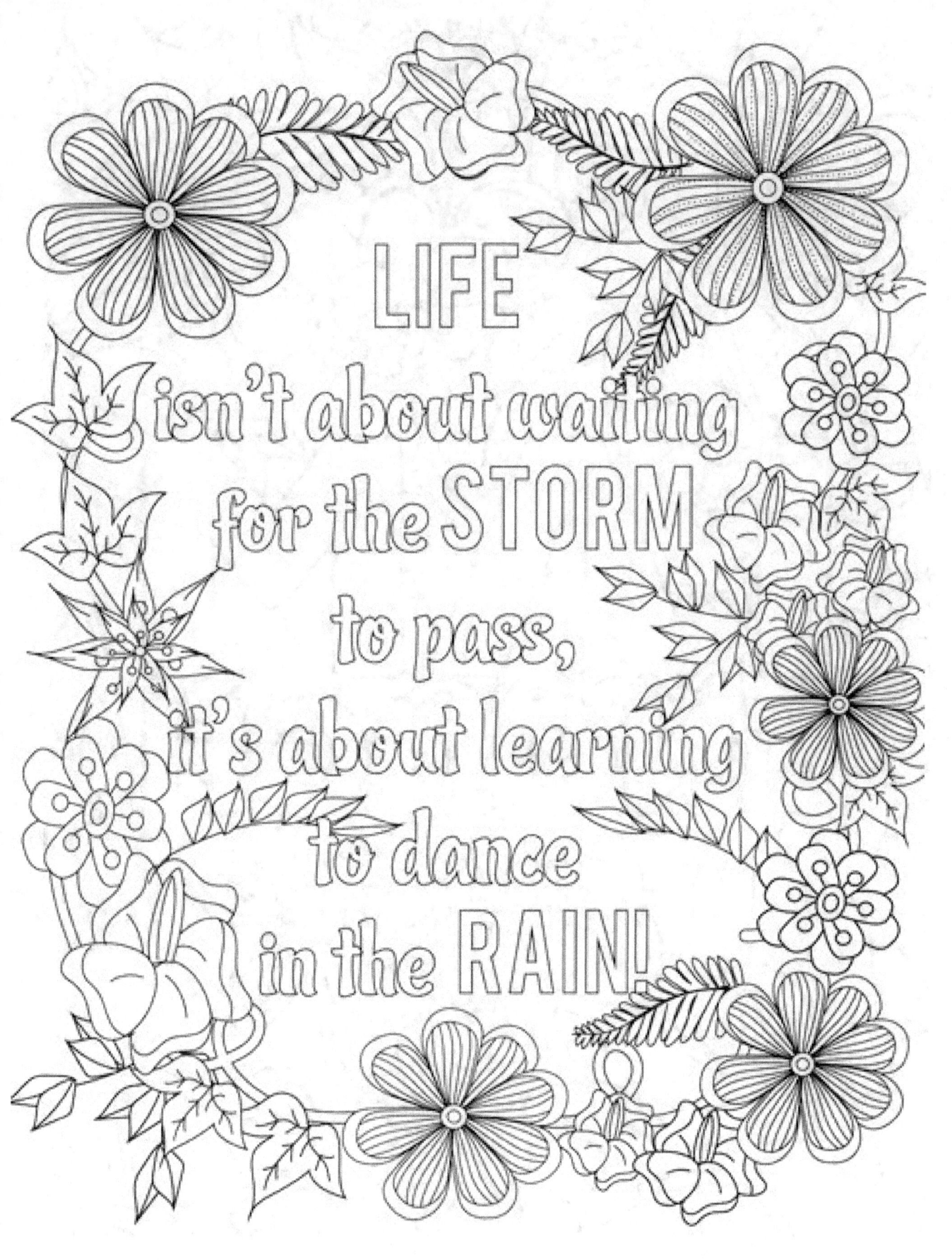

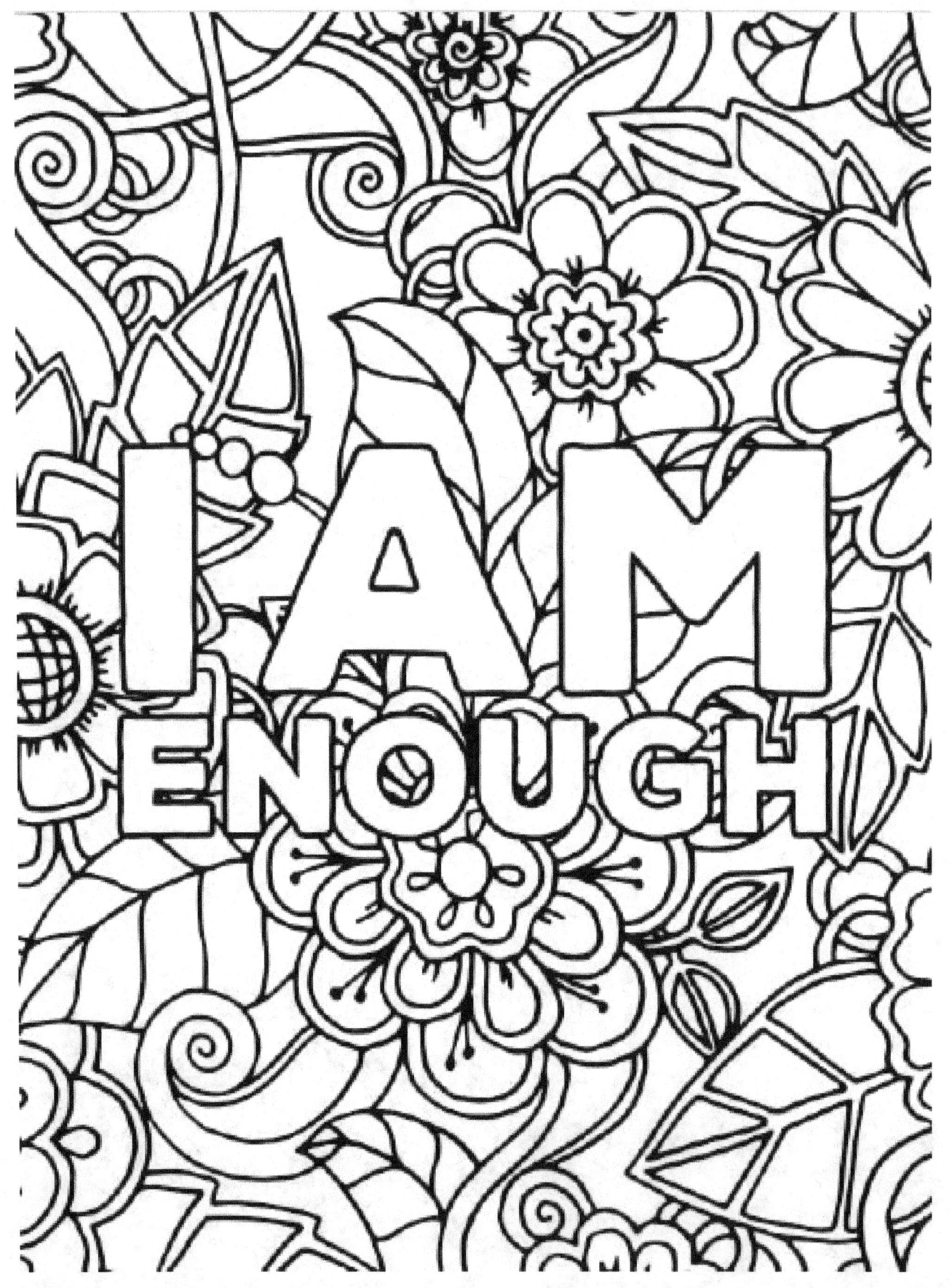

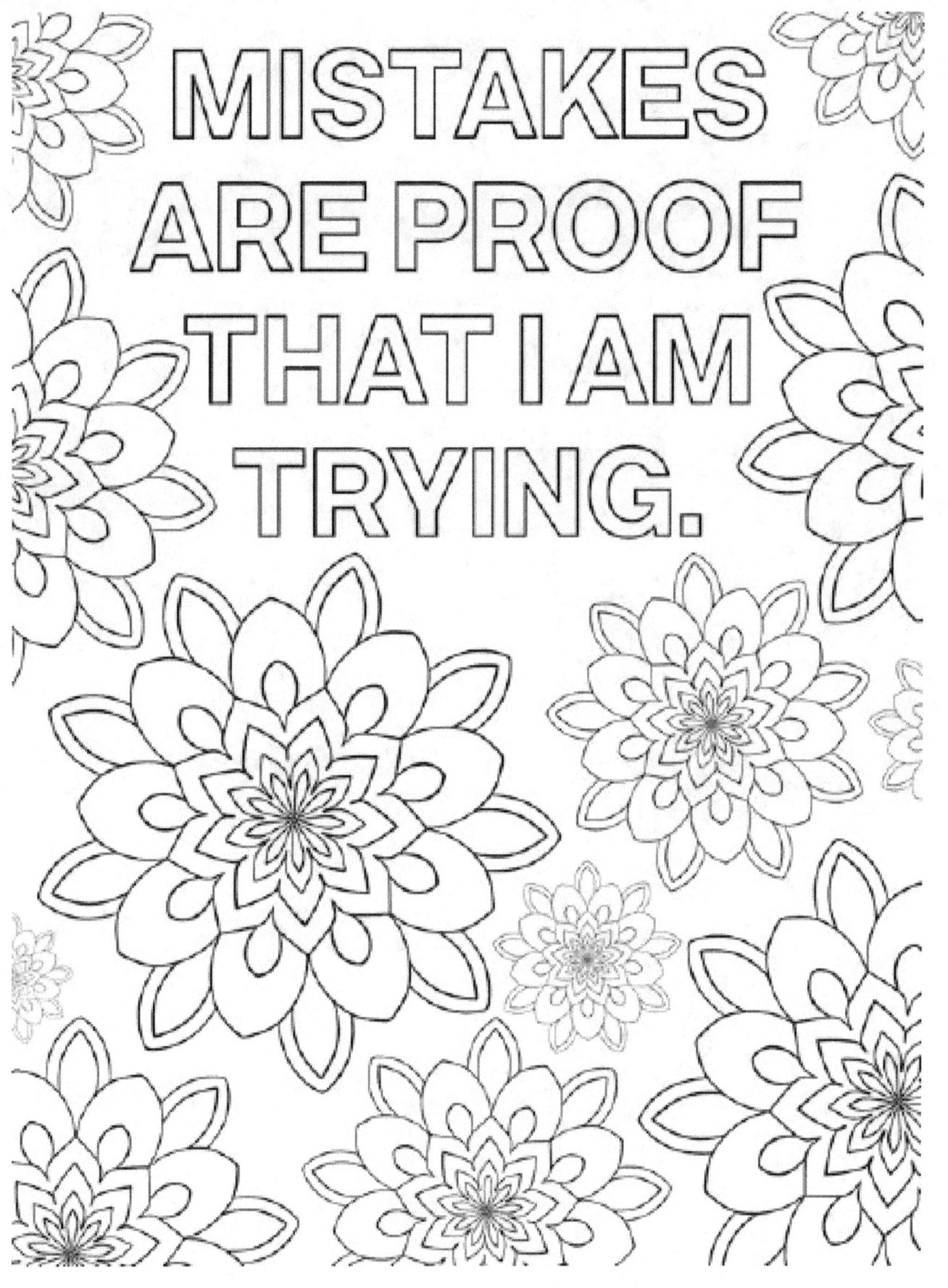

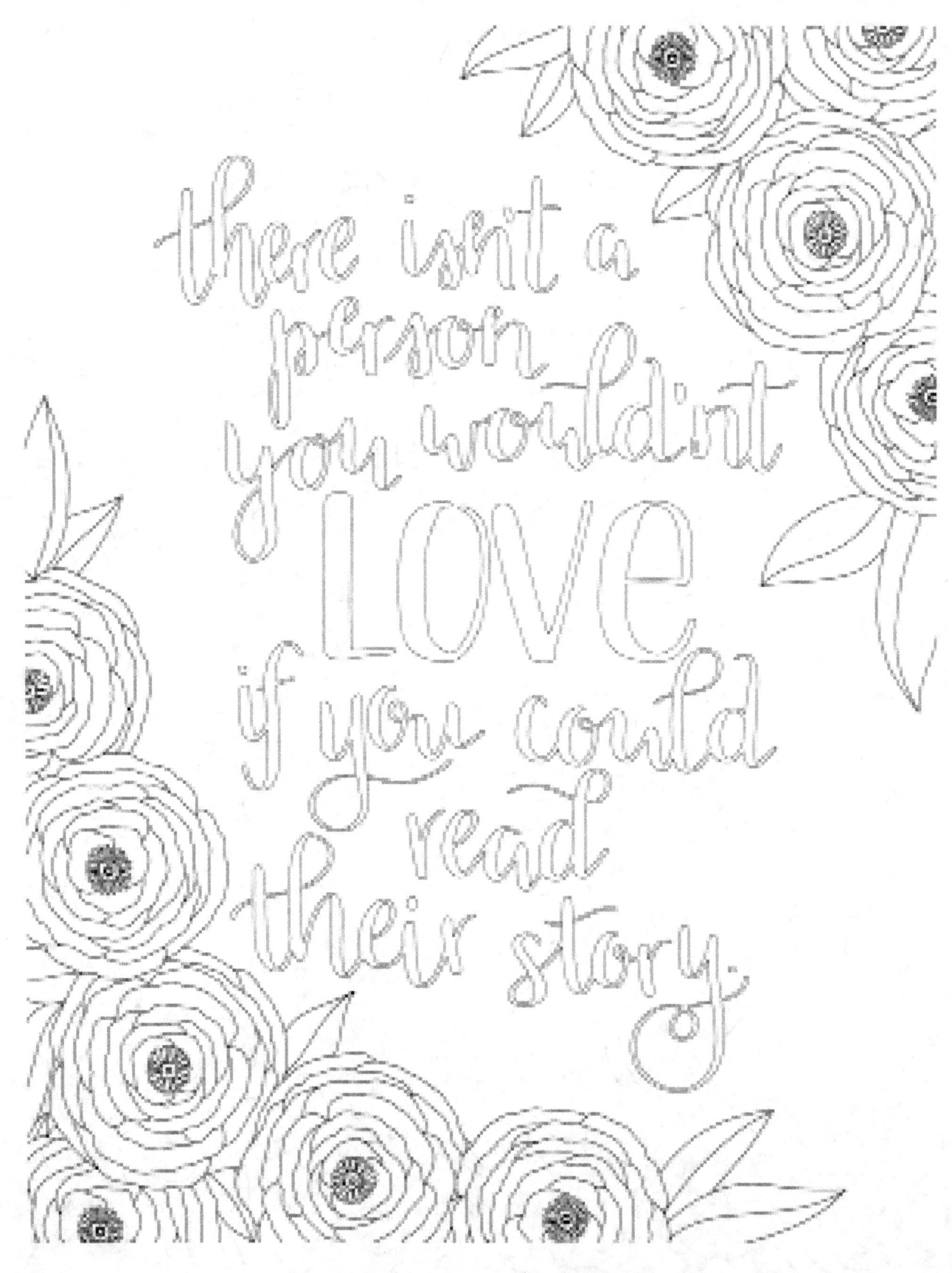

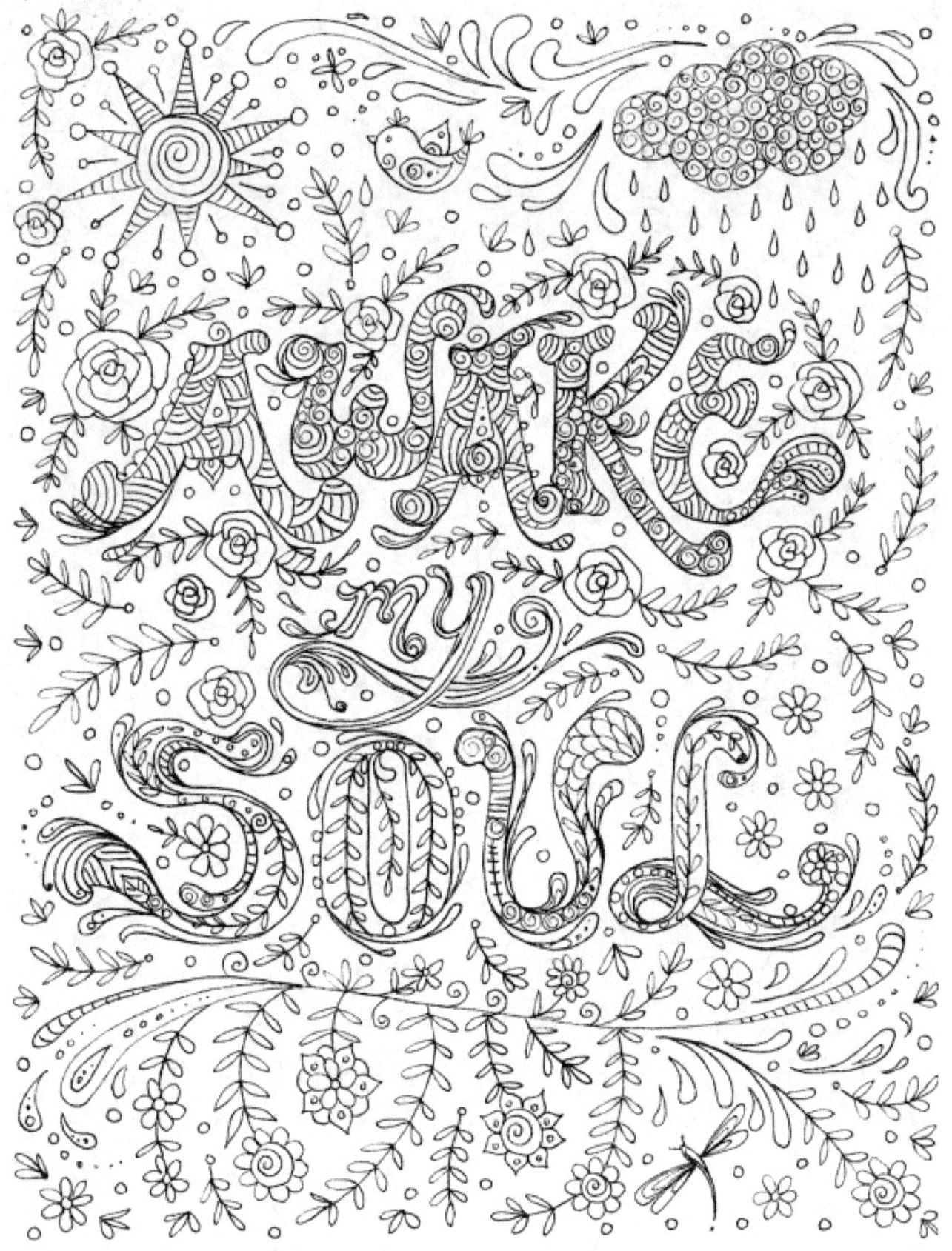

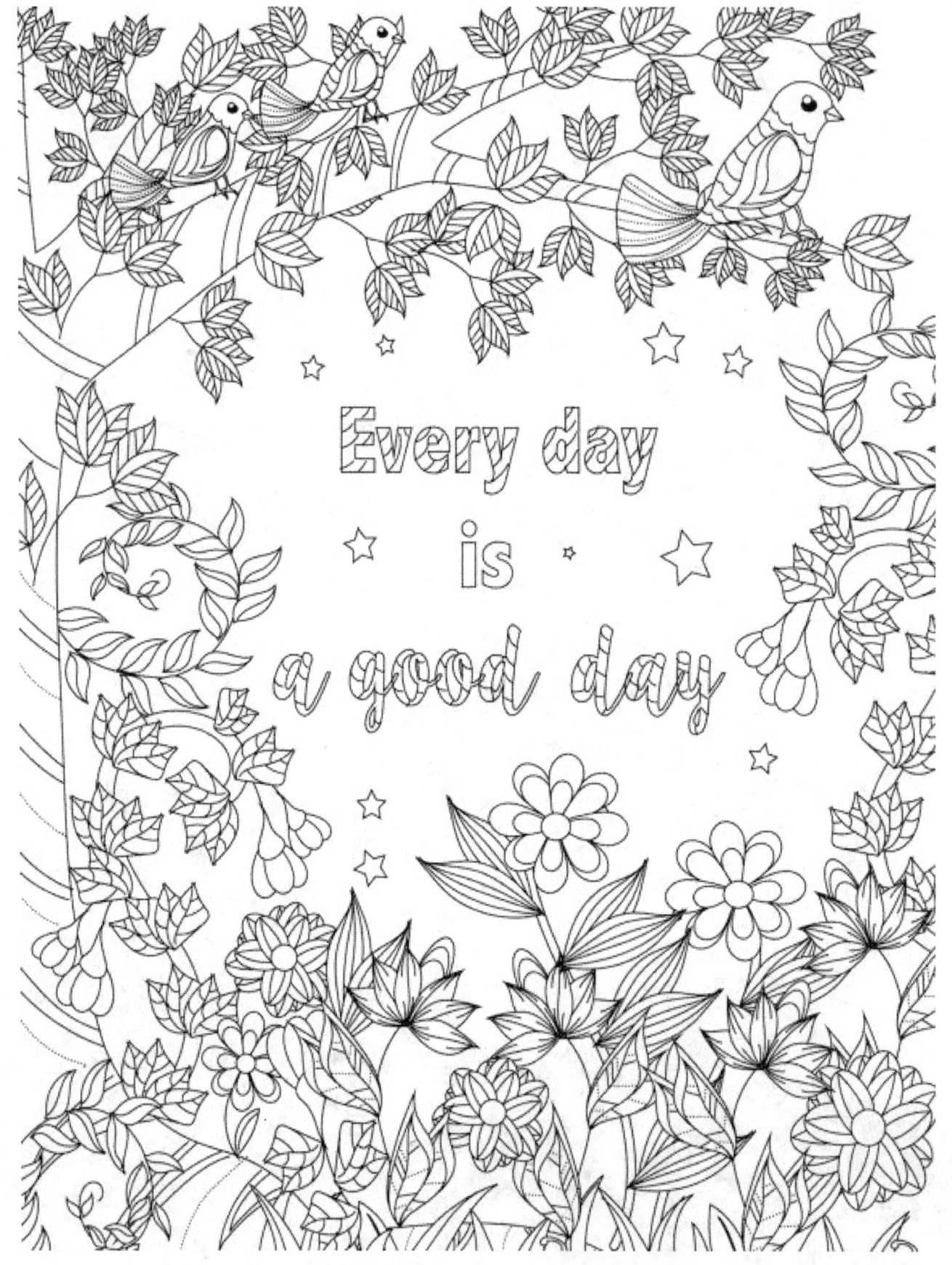

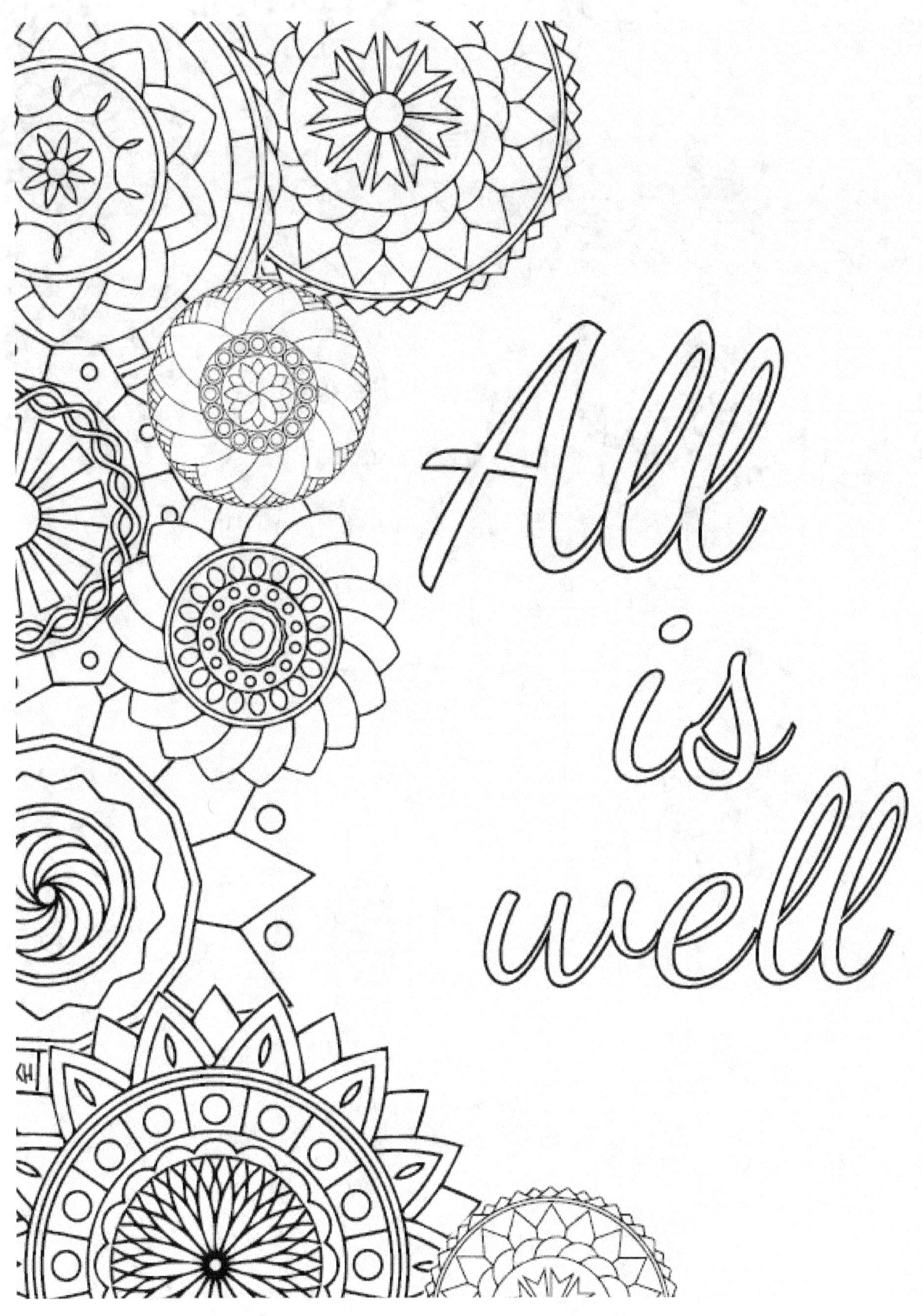

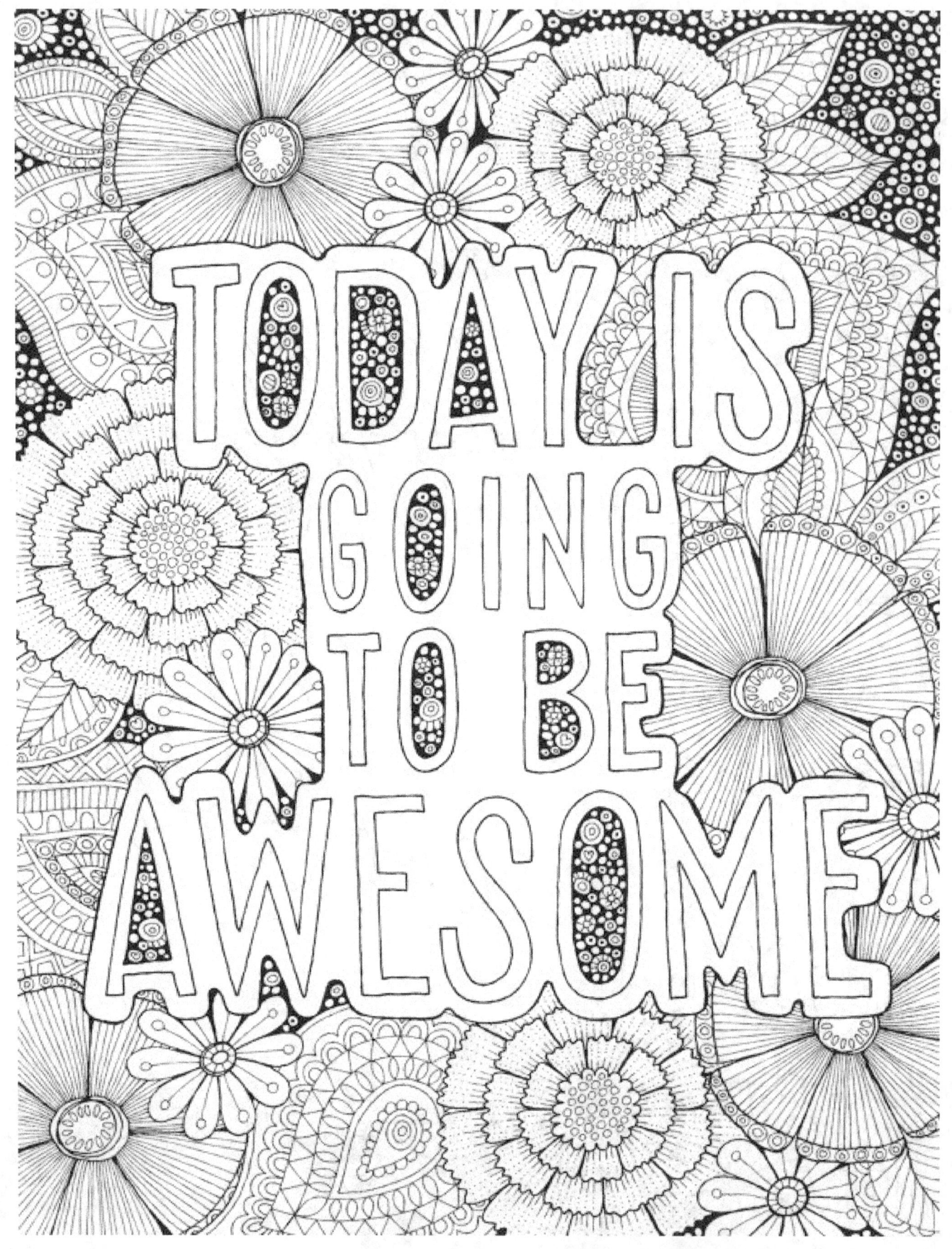

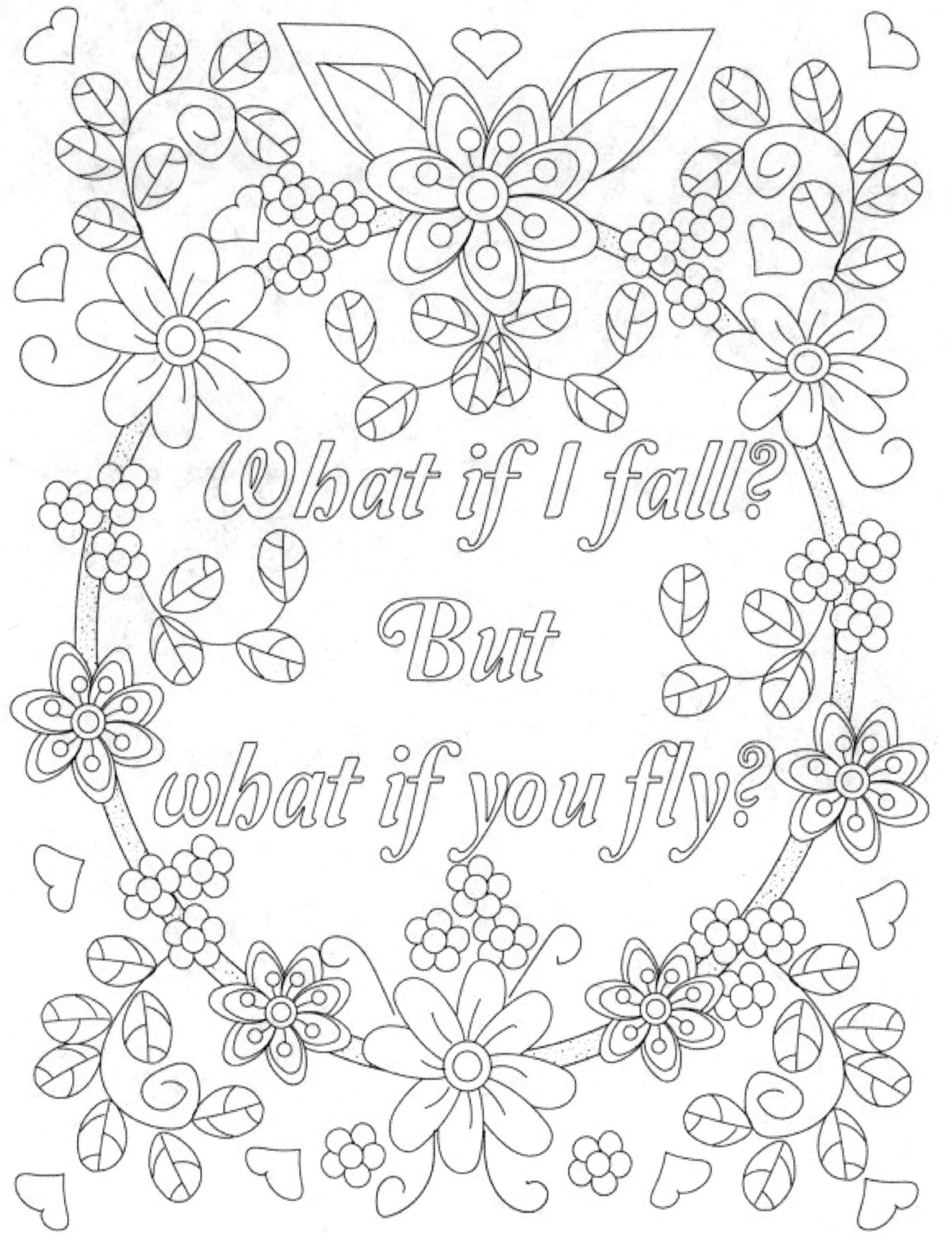

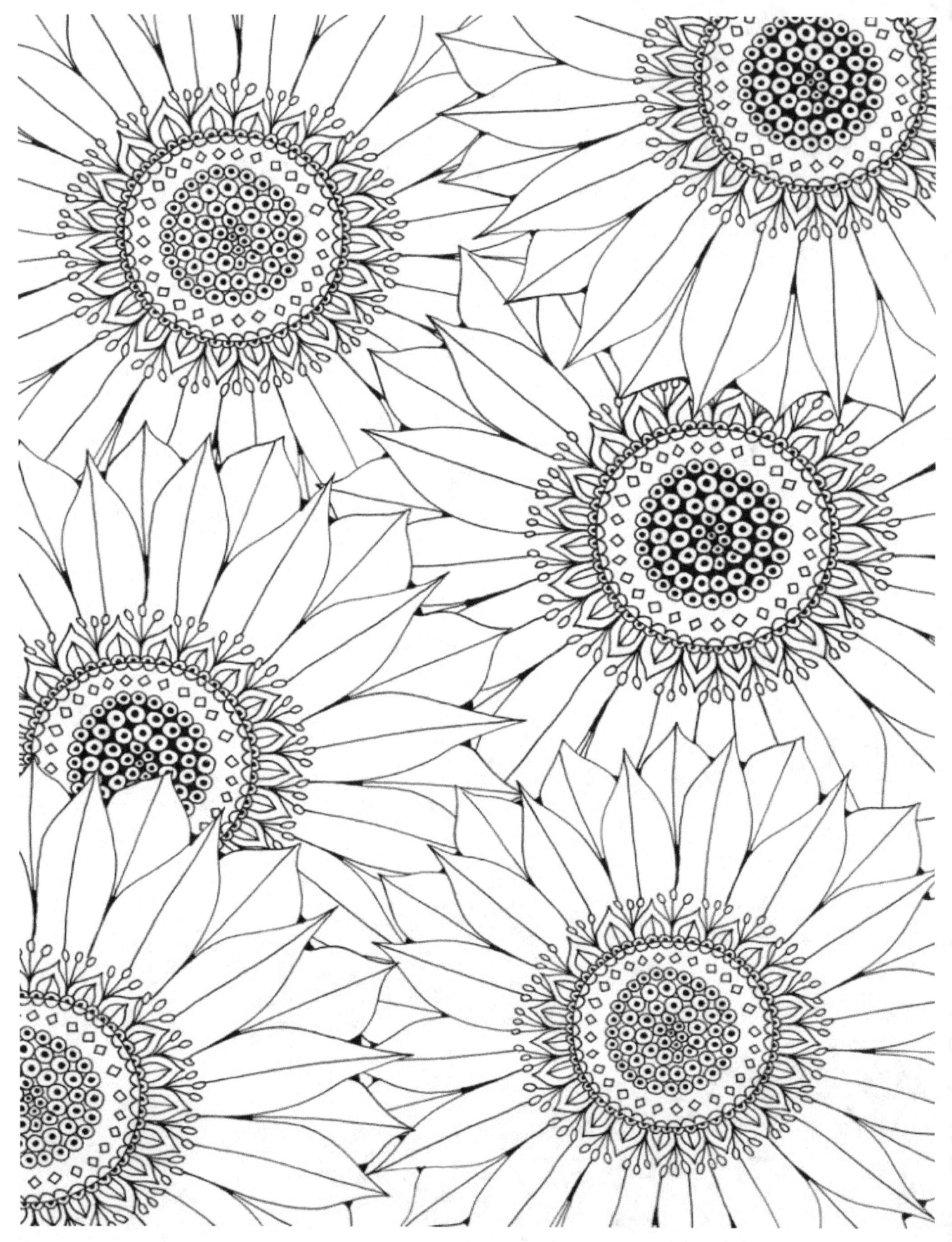

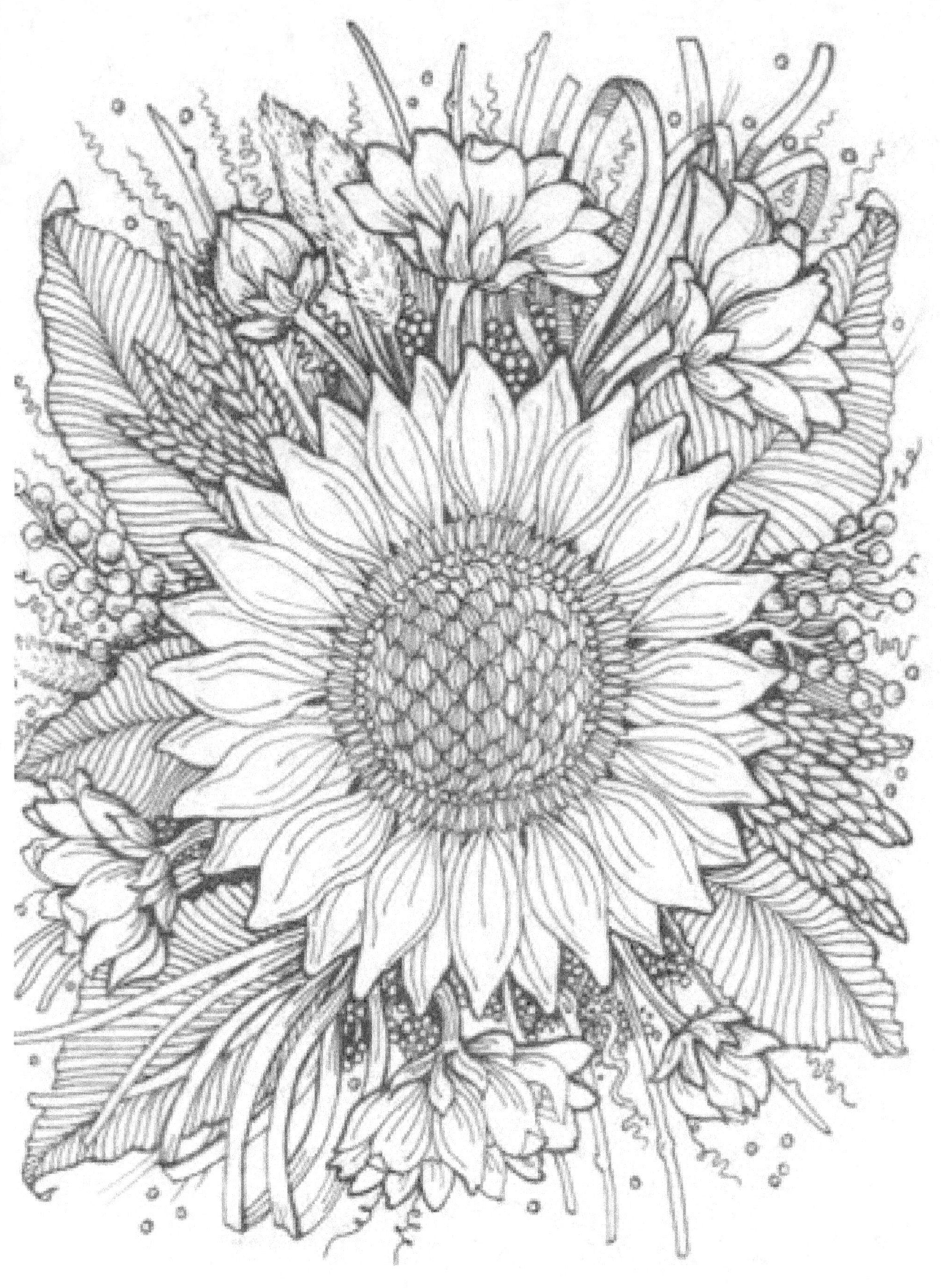

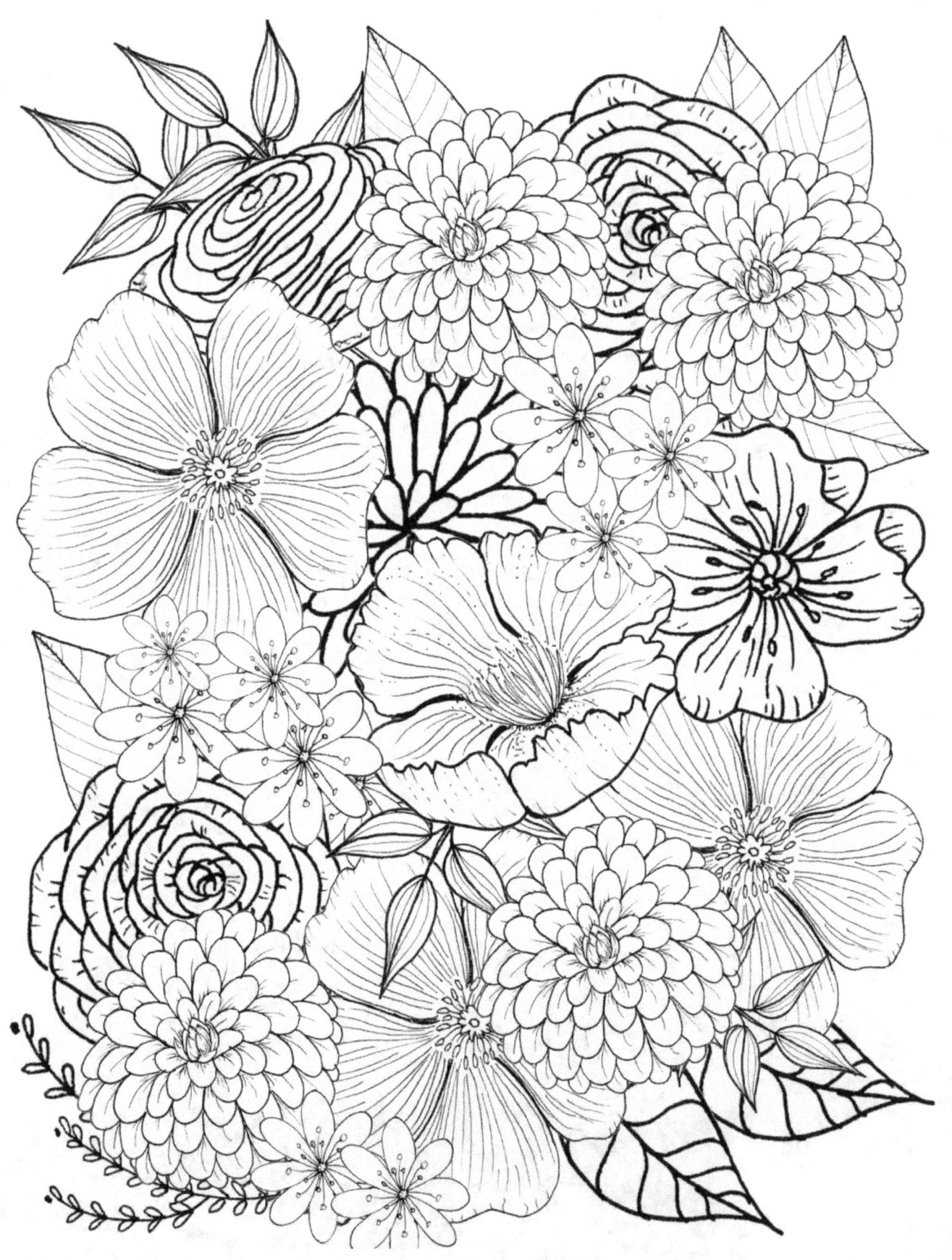

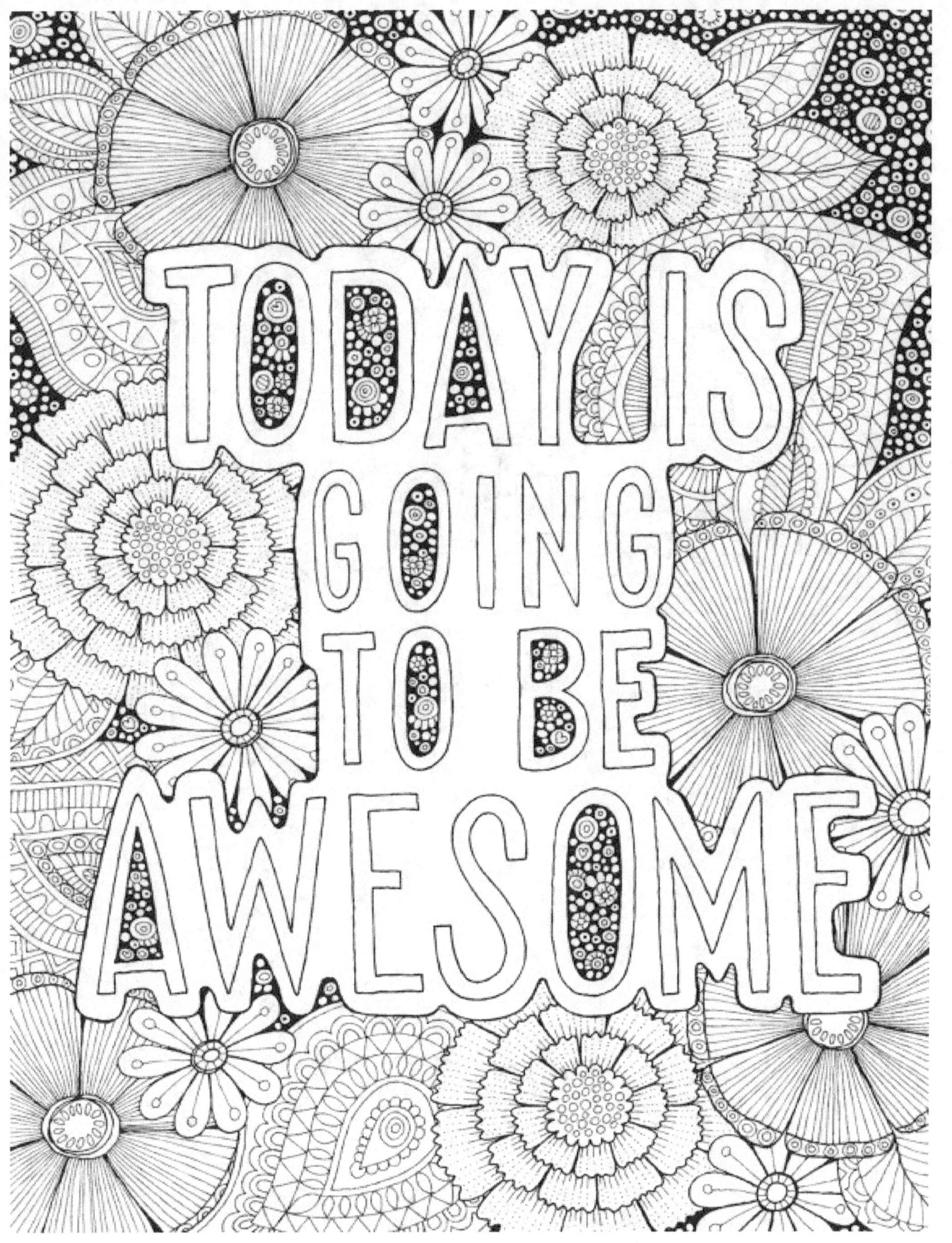

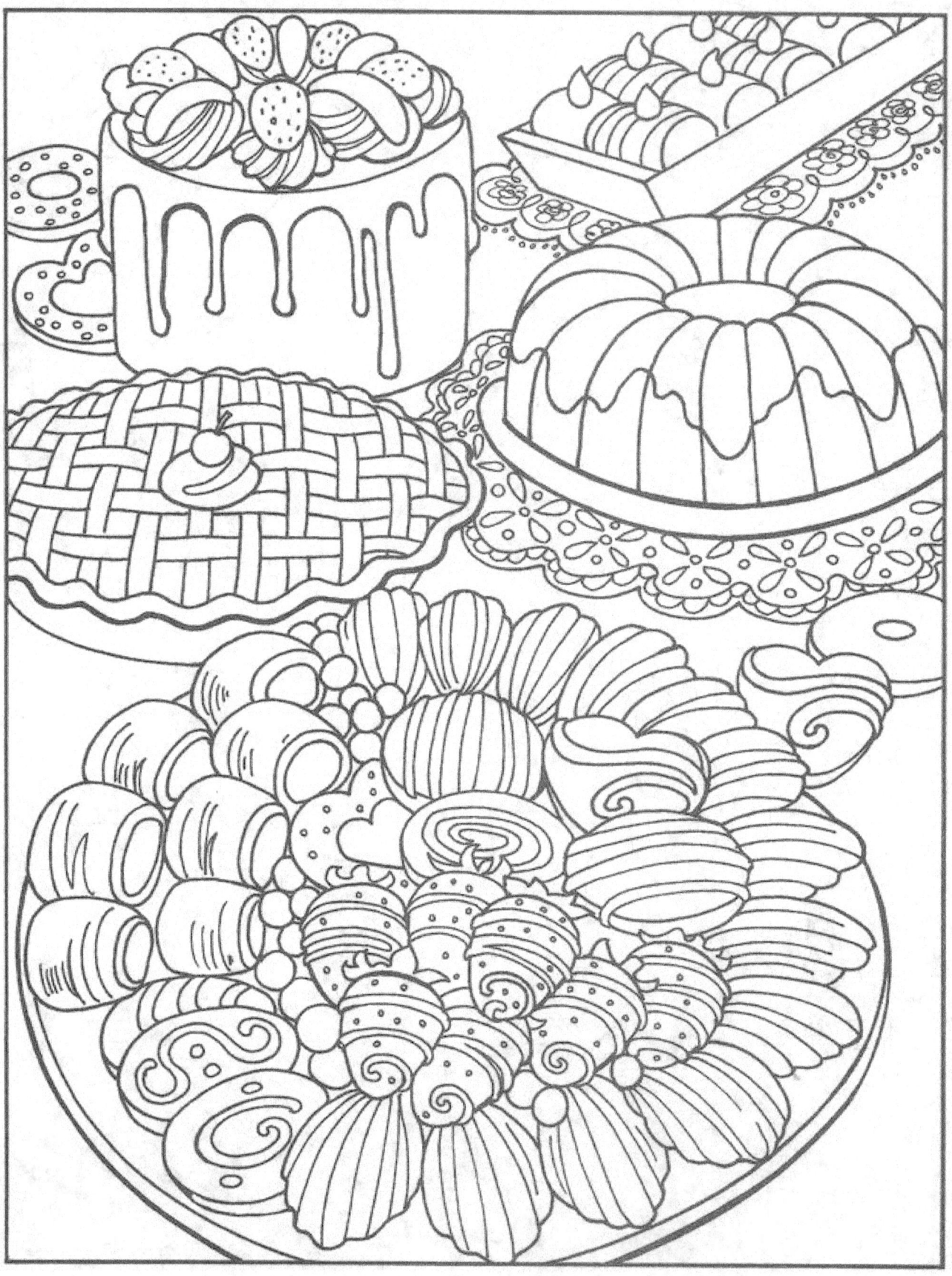

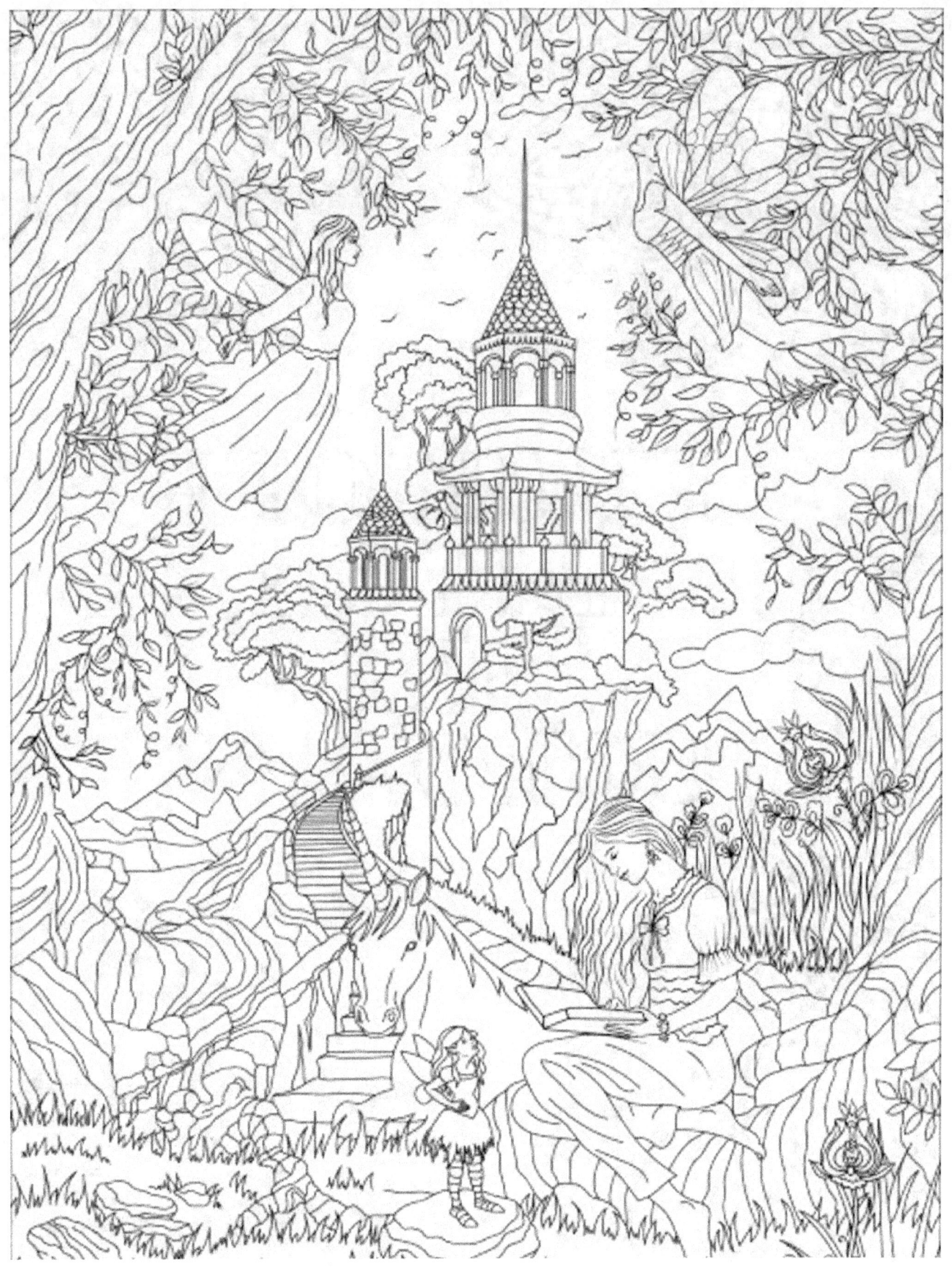

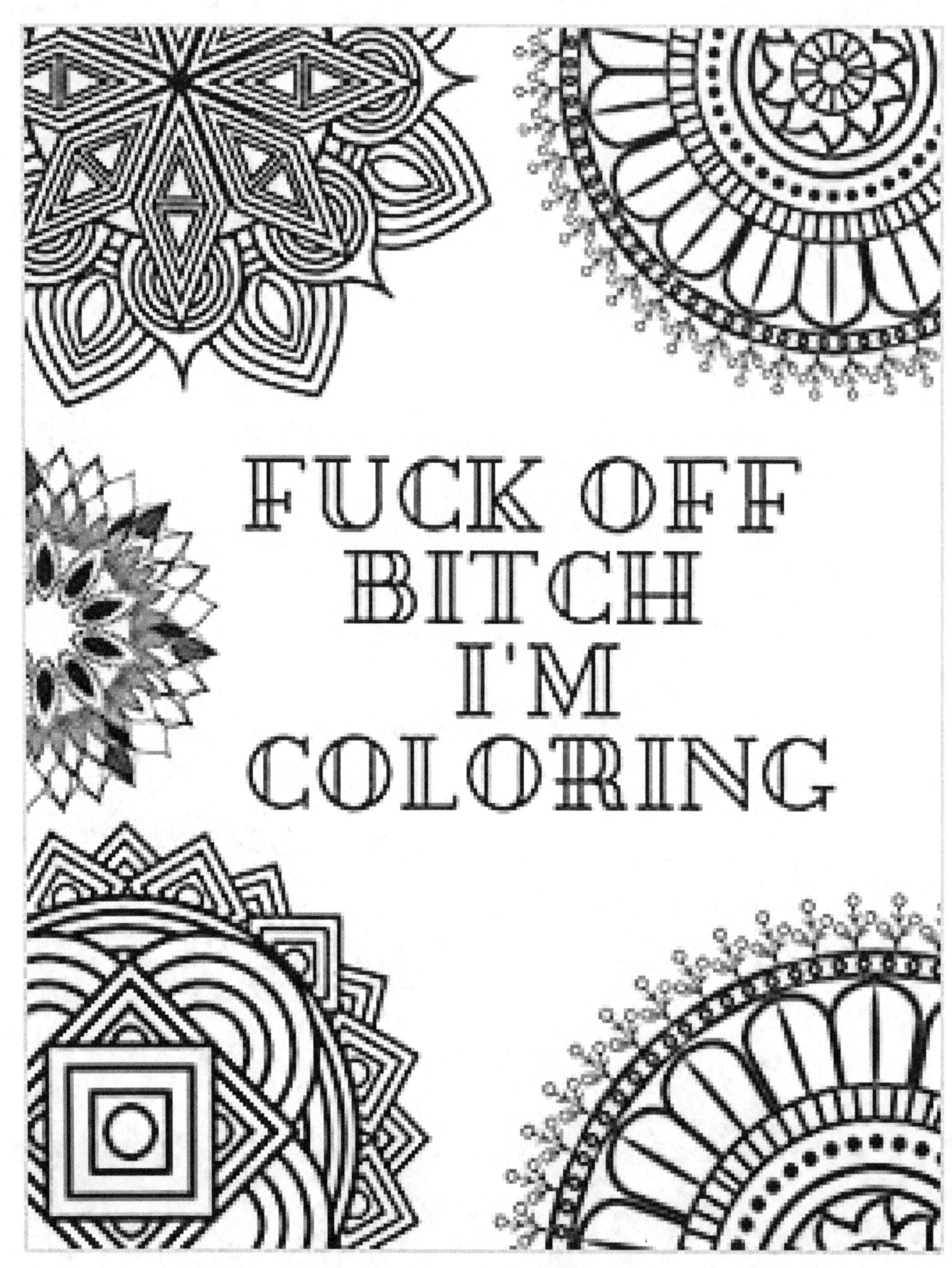

www.ingramcontent.com/pod-product-compliance
Lightning Source LLC
Chambersburg PA
CBHW081537220526
45467CB00010B/3227